May keep you. Num. 6:24

E. Dale Davis

DOES GOD CARE ABOUT YOU AND ME?

By

E. DALE DAVIS

authorHOUSE®

AuthorHouse™
1663 Liberty Drive, Suite 200
Bloomington, IN 47403
www.authorhouse.com
Phone: 1-800-839-8640

© *2009 E. Dale Davis. All rights reserved.*

No part of this book may be reproduced, stored in a retrieval system, or transmitted by any means without the written permission of the author.

First published by AuthorHouse 5/15/2009

ISBN: 978-1-4389-6920-6 (sc)
ISBN: 978-1-4389-6922-0 (hc)

Printed in the United States of America
Bloomington, Indiana

This book is printed on acid-free paper.

All Scripture quotations, unless otherwise indicated, are taken from the *New King James Version,* Copyright 1982 by Thomas Nelson, Inc., Used by permission, all rights reserved.

DEDICATION

This book is dedicated to the Glory of God and His Kingdom and to my wife, Lou N. Davis.

FAITH

Hebrews 11:1: "Faith is the substance of things hoped for, the evidence of things not seen."

What we can easily see is really only a small part of our world. We cannot see air or electricity, but we can see the results of their energy and work. Faith in Christ and our Father, God, is like that. The Holy Spirit works like that. Faith is having the vision to see what God would have us believe, become, and do. The Holy Spirit supplies the vision and power. He gives sight to our inner spirit; and we see with our brain and imagination what, when, where, and how God can use us and what He would have us do (See Eph. 1:18).

PREFACE

These messages have been written and published for the purpose of helping persons grow in the knowledge of our Lord and Savior, Jesus Christ.

There is in Is. 55:11 a great promise for all believers: "So shall My word be that goes forth from My mouth: It shall not return to Me void, but it shall accomplish what I please, and it shall prosper in the thing for which I sent it." In the New Testament is found: "Let the word of Christ dwell in you richly in all wisdom, teaching, and admonishing one another" (Col. 3:16).

It is in this spirit and with a very prayerful attitude that these messages have been written. All of us need to grow in the knowledge of God's word and to remember that that knowledge is to be closely bound to one's belief, convictions, faith, thoughts, and conduct.

Most of the references and illustrations are taken from the Bible—primarily the New Testament. The teaching and the authority of Scriptures are emphasized. The writer has attempted to avoid a sectarian approach. Instead, he has tried to present what the Scriptures actually say. Hopefully, these sermons will help individuals draw closer to their Savior and resolve to serve Him in a more steadfast way.

This author is deeply grateful to Lou N. Davis for the preparation and editing of this manuscript for publication. He is also grateful to

Thomas N. Nelson, Inc., for their permission to use *The New King James Version* of the Bible, Copyright 1979, 1980, 1982.

CONTENTS

1. God's Guidance and Provision...........................1
2. Does God Care about You and Me?......................11
3. Is Your Heart in a Far Country?...........................19
4. Broken Relationships and What Can Be Done about Them ...27
5. Spiritual Procrastination—A Major Cause of many Problems in Christian Growth and Service 37
6. Spiritual Procrastination, Part 2........................47
7. Can You Visualize This?.................................57
8. No Room for the Savior 67
9. Pre-Christmas Thoughts 77
10. Overcoming One's Mental, Spiritual, and Physical Environment..87
11. Christian Problem Solving...............................99
12. Christian Problem Solving in Human Relations 109
13. Jesus As the Way, the Truth, and the Life 119
14. Four Fruits of the Spirit in a Christian's Life................129
15. Five other Fruits of the Spirit..............................139
16. Christian Stewardship and Divine Promises................149
17. The resurrection of Jesus Christ—An Easter Message 157
18. Affirmation—Encouragement—of Ourselves and Others 167

CHAPTER 1

GOD'S GUIDANCE AND PROVISION

SCRIPTURAL BACKGROUND: Ps. 139 and Phil. 2:1-15

TEXT: Phil. 2:13 "For it is God who works in you both to will and to do for His good pleasure."

God's guidance and provision cannot be separated. By the term, God's provision, this writer means the *foreseeing care* and guardianship of God over His people. He also means God's providence—the manifestation of divine care and the fore-thought of God for His creation.

God's guidance means He gives direction, leadership, oversight, care, and assistance to believers and to those who truly seek Him and His will for their lives. The text can be better understood if one reads Phil. 2:1-15 and carefully studies the powerful verses therein. They are rich in meaning. In Verses 1 and 2 Paul urges us to be like Christ in our minds. He was always seeking the love and will of His father. He served unselfishly; we are to serve with the same mind and spirit. Just as Christ obeyed, we are to obey. Phil. 2:8b tells us: "He humbled Himself and became obedient to the point of death, even the death of the cross." Our text says it is God who works in us; and verse 12 points out that we are to work out our salvation with fear and trembling. No, this is not a gospel of salvation by works; it is rather a strong plea by Paul that once we are saved, born again in Christ, we are to work out God's gift of salvation as we do His will as Christ did. We are to seek God's will, guidance, and provision so that we can truly be "likeminded, having the same love, being of one accord, of one mind" (Phil. 2:2). Verses 3 and 4 show us how we are to live and look upon others. As we so live and serve, God's will for our lives will be revealed to us; and He will provide the strength and providence that we need (Phil. 4:6, 13). Prov. 3:6 speaks to this truth: "In all your ways acknowledge Him, and He shall direct your paths." Some of the early Hebrew manuscripts say: "He will make smooth or straight your paths."

Psalm 139 brings out some startling truths about God and those who put their trust in Him. In this Psalm David praises God for His all-seeing providence. Consider the following truths brought out by Psalm 139: God knows you and me—our past, present, and future (Verses 1-2). He knows what we do and do not do (Verse 2); our thoughts (Verse 2b); how we have lived and are living (Verse 3); what we have done and are doing—all our ways (Verse 3b); our speech—whether good or evil (Verse 4); and our limitations, talents, strengths, desires, goals, and needs (Verses 5-6).

In ancient Israel a father at times would lay his hands on a child and speak words of comfort to encourage and remind him that he was important, that he was a unique creation of God, and that God wanted him to have a special future. Today our heavenly Father can—and will—touch our lives if we seek His provision and guidance.

Again, let us remember that God knows all about us. He knows who and what we are, but He still loves us (Verses 7-9). Many people are amazed that God knows all about us—yet still loves us. They are intimidated when they hear or read the fact that He knows all of our thoughts, words, and actions; yes, and even the motives behind them.

Verses 7-9 also tell us that there is no place between heaven and hell in which we can hide from God; however, even though He knows all of the above—everything about us—He still loves and cares for us. Our text reminds us: "It is God who works in you both to will and to do for His good pleasure."

God holds us in His hands—His care and provision; and He can lead and guide us by His "right hand" (Verse 10). When we feel lost, lonely, down-hearted, and like worthless losers; the One who knows us even better than we know ourselves is ready and willing to place us in His care—to hold, guide, and lead us every single moment. Thus our prayer should be: "Show me Your ways, O Lord; Teach me Your paths. Lead me in Your truth and teach me, For You are the God of my salvation; on You I wait all the day" (Ps. 25:4-5).

God protects us in the dark, sad, discouraging times of our lives (Ps. 139:11-12). We worry about present problems; that which burdens us down in the shadows of life; we fear the unknown and the unexpected in the future. God's word tells us in another Psalm of David: "I sought the Lord, and He heard me, And delivered me from all my fears" (Ps. 34:4). Verse 7 of the same Psalm speaks to our quest for God's provision and guidance: "The angel of the Lord encamps all around those who fear Him; And delivers them." Verses 8b, 9b, and 10b say: "Blessed is the man who trusts in Him! ...There is no want to those who fear Him. ...those who seek the Lord shall not lack any good thing."

God made you a unique person. There is no one else exactly like you—no one who thinks, serves, dreams, and hopes for exactly the same things you do. He planned every aspect of you and your life. You are not a *nobody*. You were custom designed—"you" are the only "you" that God ever made (Ps. 139:13-16). Again, our text tells us: "For it is God who works in you." God has a plan for your life. Verses 16b-18 assure it. He has ordained your days—the length of your life, and His plan for it. This was done even before you were born. Yes, this does stagger the thinking processes.

God hears our prayers for help, guidance, direction, worship, and service (Verse 19-22). Sometimes His presence makes the way sure and easy. At other times we cry out for help, provision, and guidance; and the answers are slow in coming. Yet, we are to trust Him and His providence. He knows us, our needs, and what is best for us. That is the reason we pray for His will, not ours, to be done. Phil. 2:13: "It is God who works in you both to will and to do for His good pleasure."

When we pray and cry out for help and for God to look upon our lives and needs, He hears us (Ps. 139:23-24). God loves us in spite of the fact that He knows us through and through. We must ask Him to search our hearts for any wickedness; and we must prayerfully, sincerely, ask for Him to forgive us of our sins and to cleanse us from anything that is unrighteous. Then it is that God's care, provision, help, and guidance will come into our minds, hearts, and lives. Then as we pray: "Your will be done," He can manifest His will and plan for our lives. His providence, foreseeing care, and guardianship are thus able to function in our lives. His divine presence can and will provide guidance. Again, "It is God who works in you."

In the above paragraphs, using Psalm 139, this writer has tried to show that God loves, cares for, and seeks to guide those who in faith and belief sincerely look to Him. He is not an absentee spirit; He does not hide His concern for humans. All through the Old Testament He declares His love and concern for His people. In the New Testament He continues His care and providence, and this is shown in a mighty way with the sending of His Son and the Holy Spirit. Jesus, our Savior, promises that if we abide in Him and ask in His name, He will provide for us and guide us with the Holy Spirit. One hundred years ago C. D. Martin wrote a hymn that summarizes much of the above, and W. S.

Martin set it to music. The name of the hymn is "God Will Take Care of You." It is still sung in many churches. This writer memorized it as a teenager. The first stanza goes this way:

"Be not dismayed whate'er betide, God will take care of you:
Beneath His wings of love abide, God will take care of you."

At this point in the message it is important to consider the question: How can we discover God's will and guidance in our everyday walk of life? The first thing I think we must believe is that truly God has a plan for our lives, as stated earlier. It is up to us to find that plan by believing that through faith, prayer, and willingness to live for Him, He will guide us. There is another hymn that speaks to this truth. It was written by Peter and William Williams in the 18th century. The first stanza is as follows:

"Guide me, O Thou great Jehovah, Pilgrim through this barren land;
I am weak, but thou art mighty, Hold me with Thy powerful hand;
Bread of heaven, Feed me till I want no more."

To be more specific, this writer makes the following suggestions which are based on his study of the Scriptures:

> Pray for God's leadership and guidance.
>
> Trust God—His provision and providence. Remember Christ is at this very moment making intercessory prayer for you at His Father's throne. *Trust and obey,* as the hymn states.
>
> Ask God to take charge of your life and supply your needed guidance and help. Ask Him to take your will and make it in keeping with His will. Remember He knows even when a sparrow falls, and He stands ready to help when we seek His will.
>
> Through prayer surrender every facet of your life, every need, and every goal to Him. In Luke 6:47-48 Christ spoke, saying: "Whoever comes to Me, and hears My sayings and

does them, I will show you whom he is like: He is like a man building a house, who dug deep and laid the foundation on the rock. And when the flood arose, the stream beat vehemently against that house, and could not shake it, for it was founded on the rock." If you are confused, feel defeated, overcome with sorrow and strife, then do "tell it to Jesus." Tell Him you want His help and that you want to start over. He is willing to help and guide you. Remember "it is God who works in you both to will and to do for His good pleasure."

Always keep in mind that God guides through His holy word. Do not pray for something that His word forbids (especially in His ten commandments and the great teachings Christ gives in Matthew, Chapters 5-7).

Pray for spiritual strength to resist temptations, for a greater faith, and for a deeper relationship with Christ, our Savior and Lord. Study His word to increase your faith and to resist evil.

Pray for that which has a biblical basis and not for those things which concern only worldly affairs. Memorize the Model Prayer Christ gave to us in Mt. 6:9-13. Use it as a guide, and pray for others as much as you do for yourself. Pray especially for your family, friends, fellow Christians, the sick, those with whom you work, for our nation, the armed forces, and for those who serve as missionaries.

Pray for guidance in doing those things that will serve to glorify Christ's name and extend His kingdom and message of love and service.

Pray for God's guidance and provision that you will know and express true Christian love; and that however He leads, you will be able to do good for Him and for the people whose lives are affected by you.

Pray that God's response to your prayers will lead you to an inner assurance of conviction that that which you seek—His provision and guidance—is the course of action you should follow. This feeling of assurance may be the stimulus to venture out in faith. Remember "faith is the substance of things hoped for, the evidence of things not seen" (Heb. 11:1). In many things for which we pray we must venture out in faith, not knowing all the answers; however, God has given us a mind. Thus we can ask questions of Him and ourselves. Some of these might be as follows:

   a. Will it help me to be a more obedient Christian?
   b. Will it help build His kingdom and my Christian witness?
   c. Will it be something that now and in the future I can thank and praise Christ for His help and leadership in? (Will it be in keeping with our text: "It is God who works in you")?
   d. Will it be challenging and important enough really to require my best efforts and God's help to accomplish it? In other words, is it something of importance for me and others?
   e. Will it be in keeping with my Christian conduct and convictions? If so, truly one can say: "It is God who works in me."

Pray that it will be in keeping with your desire to love God and His people and serve His church (His called out believers).

Pray that it will help you "grow in the grace and knowledge of your Lord and Savior, Jesus Christ" (2 Pet. 3:18a). If God's guidance and provision supply this, will it glorify Him and help you to be a more effective, challenged Christian to use your abilities and opportunities for Him and His work?

Pray that it can be done without anxiety, worry, and fear; and that it can be Asked in unselfish "supplication, with thanksgiving" (Phil. 4:6b). If it can, then you can believe that "it is God who works in you both to will and to do for His good pleasure."

Pray about the demands it will make on your financial resources. Can you afford it and still be a faithful steward to God's church, your family, and to others who are in need? If it takes away the funds you must use for these three things, be very slow to attempt it.

This writer feels very deeply about praying with all sincerity concerning the above suggestions. They are to him *guidelines*—guidelines that are important for seeking God's guidance and provision in daily living. Many outstanding Christian writers have set forth their guidelines and questions for seeking God's will. One of the best this writer has encountered is found in Ogilvie's *Silent Strength for My Life*.[1] The writings of Billy Graham, and especially his *Hope for Each Day*, contain many suggestions for seeking and finding God's guidance and provision.[2] Yet, it is important that you study God's word and make and use your own list. At least prayerfully think of the factors listed above and stated in other books. Always think: Will it be "God who works in you" if your prayers are answered?

Let it be clearly understood that prayer and the Bible are of utmost importance. God is a Spirit, and we must worship Him in spirit and in truth. As we undertake to know God's will for our lives and as we pray for His provision and guidance, there are several other most important factors that should be carefully considered. The first is to remember we are called out to obey God' word and to do *His* will, not our own.

This means that it is fundamental for us to turn our backs on any sin or practice that we know is wrong, harmful, and clearly destructive of close fellowship with Christ. We must renounce, give up, and abandon any element in our daily living that interferes with communion with our Lord. How can we expect God to guide and provide for us if our lives are not free from sins we know are contrary to His word and will?

In an earlier century the famous minister, Charles Spurgeon, stressed in many of his sermons and teachings that obedience, faith, and prayer are all three tied together. His position was that a Christian who obeys his Lord will trust Him; and one who trusts Him will obey Him and His word. Thus we are to keep our minds and hearts open and in complete trust that God in His great power and knowledge will guide, provide, and lead us in the decisions, opportunities, and actions that will result in our knowing His will for our lives. It is then possible for His continued providence and power to guide and sustain us in the way He would have us go.

There is another important factor in God's guidance and provision. Our prayers and God's provision may demand that we wait on the Lord—yes, even that we wait patiently on Him. Ogilvie calls this waiting *lead time*, and so it is.[3] He also points out what Paul had to say about consistent prayer and praise. In 1 Thess. 5:16-18a we find these words: "Rejoice always, pray without ceasing, in everything give thanks." Also in Phil. 4:4 and 6 we read: "Rejoice in the Lord always. Again I will say, rejoice!" "Be anxious for nothing, but in everything by prayer and supplication, with thanksgiving, let your requests be made known to God." We are to be consistent in living our convictions, constantly rejoicing and praising God for His mercy and manifold blessings—His providence and guidance in the past. We are to pray and wait on the Lord: and we are to trust Him for guidance, timing, and answers to our prayers. Thus we then can realize: "It is God who works in you."

CHAPTER 2

DOES GOD CARE ABOUT YOU AND ME?

SCRIPTURAL BACKGROUND: Mt. 6:25-34 and 1 Pet. 5:6-11

TEXT: 1 Pet. 5:7 "Casting all your care upon Him, for He cares for you."

In the previous message this writer attempted to set forth *some* of the biblical truths about God's guidance and providence. He used Psalm 139 to show the following:

    God knows us—better than we know ourselves.

    He is always aware of our actions.

    He is aware of our thoughts and motives.

    He is aware of how we live our lives.

    He knows every word we speak—even before we speak it.

    He knows what words and encouragement we need to hear.

    He loves us—with an everlasting love.

    He cares for us and encourages us to abide in Him.

    He considers us of great value—even when we feel downcast, confused, and unworthy. God gave His Son for us.

    He offers His constant presence, protection, mercy, and grace to us at all times.

He designed us and gave us physical life and the hope of eternal life in Christ.

God offers all of the above to believers who trust in His Son. But there is more.

He offers His providence, foreseeing care, and guardianship to all who "will trust and obey." Devout Christians receive direction, help, and guidance from their Maker, Savior, and Lord. This gives meaning to their existence and assures that their days are ordained by God, and that He cares for them. It gives significant spiritual meaning to life in Christ. It makes one remember that believers in Christ are children of the living God, that he is their heavenly Father (1 John 3:1), and that He cares for them. In today's world which is so troubled by crime, dishonesty, corruption, and sin, the words of the Psalmist in Ps. 34:4 gives advice which needs to be heeded and followed: "I sought the Lord, and He heard me, And delivered me from all my fears." Job, after great losses and suffering, stated: "Though He slay me, yet will I trust Him" (Job 13:15a).

These verses of Scripture from the Old Testament are in keeping with our text: "Casting all your care upon Him, for He cares for you." They are also in keeping with the teachings of Jesus in the New Testament in which He stressed that we are not to fear and worry about our futures. Mt. 6:25-26 states it very well: "...do not worry about your life, what you will eat or what you will drink; nor about your body, what you will put on. Is not life more than food and the body more than clothing? Look at the birds of the air...your heavenly Father feeds them. Are you not of more value than they?" In Verses 28-33 Jesus stressed the uselessness of worry about the future and worldly things; then in Verse 34a He summarized by saying: "Therefore do not worry about tomorrow..." Notice that Jesus did not say that we should show no concern or not plan for tomorrow. In Verses 32b-34 He stated: "For your heavenly Father knows that you need all these things. But seek first the kingdom of God and His righteousness, and all these things shall be added to you. Therefore do not worry about tomorrow, for tomorrow will worry about its own things. Sufficient for the day is its own trouble."

But often in our minds and hearts we have questions. For example, persons who have afflictions or those who have been hurt in accidents ask: "Why did this happen to me?" Parents of children who fall into crime, harmful addictions, and other life problems wonder: "Why did God allow this to happen to my loved ones?" This is especially true when the parents or other providers have seriously tried to teach their offspring basic biblical truths.

There are many other factors in life that can prompt us to question the Christian truths stated in the previous message and restated above. Do the Scriptures have something to say about this? Most assuredly they do; but let this writer forcefully state that he does not have all the answers, and that he, too, often prays: "Lord, enlighten my understanding, increase my faith, and help me to trust you more." Then he is reminded that faith and belief are based on what God says in His word and on one's trust and daily walk with the Lord. Thus we can turn to Him in prayer and to His word for help, understanding, and peace. In Heb. 13:5b-6 are found these comforting words: "For He Himself has said, 'I will never leave you nor forsake you.' So that we may boldly say: 'The Lord is my helper; I will not fear'." Think of this. It is not some casual statement made by a human being. It is an inspiring promise and affirmation made by God Himself to all believers who have put their faith and trust in Christ. Psalm 118:5a says: "I called on the Lord in distress; The Lord answered me"; and in Verse 6 it continues: "The Lord is on my side; I will not fear." Jesus' final words to His disciples and other believers were "and lo, I am with you always, even to the end of the age" (Mt. 28:20b).

Thinking of Christ, His presence, and words, Joseph Scriven in the 19th Century wrote *What a Friend We Have in Jesus.* The first and second stanzas state:

> "What a friend we have in Jesus, All our sins and griefs to bear!
> What a privilege to carry Everything to God in prayer.
> Have we trials and temptations? Is there trouble anywhere?
> We should never be discouraged, Take it to the Lord in prayer."

The Scriptures quoted above and many others make it very clear that God is aware of us, our troubles, conditions, and needs. As was stated earlier, He knows us better than we know ourselves, and we can say with George Keith in his hymn, *How Firm a Foundation*:

> "When thro' the deep waters I call thee to go,
> The rivers of sorrow shall not overflow;
> For I will be with thee thy trials to bless,
> And sanctify to thee thy deepest distress."

Yet we are human and many times weak, lonely, distressed, discouraged, and confused. Still His words stand true: "I will never leave you nor forsake you" (Heb. 13:5b). J. H. Newman, in a sorrowful and discouraging time in his life, took stock of his past—much of which he regretted—and wrote these words:

> "Lead, kindly light, amid th' encircling gloom,
> Lead Thou me on; The night is dark, and I am far from home;
> Lead Thou me on: Keep Thou my feet; I do not ask to see
> The distant scene,--one step enough for me."

The Scriptures and hymns quoted above are included here because all of us need the assurance that God cares, guides, loves, and is ever near to comfort, sustain, and help us. Remember Christ promised always to be with us, and He also promised and did send the *Helper*—the Holy Spirit.

Is it any wonder then that Paul tells us in Phil. 2:1-2: "Therefore if there is any consolation in Christ, if any comfort of love, if any fellowship of the Spirit, if any affection and mercy, fulfill my joy by being like-minded, having the same love, being of one accord, of one mind." In other words, as stated in Phil. 2:5: "Let this mind be in you which was also in Christ Jesus." Christians are to face each day in whatever situation they find themselves, knowing that Christ is with them and that they are to function as His children, His servants, His representatives; knowing that whether it be sickness, death, pain or suffering, poverty or riches, distress or happiness, God is with them. Peter stated it well in 1 Pet. 5:7: "Casting all your care on Him, for He cares for you."

In the next few pages, let us prayerfully consider some of the specific characteristics that demonstrate God's care for us. The first one this writer would set forth is that Christ is God's Son. "Yes," you say, "I know this." Good! This writer is grateful that you can say so with mental and spiritual understanding of what this means. Jesus Christ is the promised Messiah. He is Emmanuel—God with us. He is the Savior and Lord sent from God, the One who came into the world not "to condemn the world, but that the world through Him might be saved" (John 3:17b). This is the basis of all evidence that God cares for us. Jesus Christ shows us that God has always cared for us. He is, as John in his gospel, states: "Behold! The Lamb of God who takes away the sin of the world" (John 1:29b). This is the fact and major reason Peter could say: "Casting all your care upon Him, for He cares for you" (1 Pet. 5:7).

Christ is also the Great Physician. John 5:8 gives just one example of the many times Jesus went about ministering to the physical and spiritual needs of people. Today Jesus can and does heal. This writer has experienced this in his own life as well as the lives of others. He has had to battle the affliction of trigeminal neuralgia, a disorder of unilateral facial pain. Doctors are not sure what causes this pain, but they suspect it results from pressure on the trigeminal nerve. The point to be made here is that for several years doctors diagnosed this condition as sinus infection, and the excruciating pain required very strong medication which prevented him from doing any type of work or public speaking. Relief was found only when a neurosurgeon performed a surgical procedure that stopped the pain and suffering. Why bring this personal reference into this message? Because it is just one more illustration of God's power and concern. God used the skill and knowledge of the surgeon to relieve the pain, thus allowing this person to resume study, writing, and work. Christ has done such healing for thousands of others. He can heal with or without modern medicine, but he certainly heals in both ways.

Jesus does care, and we can heed and believe the words of our text: "Casting all your care upon Him, for He cares for you." In Mt. 6:25-27 Christ says: "Do not worry about your life, what you will eat or what you will drink; nor about your body, what you will put on….Look at the birds of the air…your heavenly Father feeds them. Are you not of more value than they? Which of you by worrying can add one cubit to his stature?" And Mt. 6:30-34 states: "Now if God so clothes the grass of the field, which today is, and tomorrow is thrown into the oven, will He not much more clothe you? …therefore do not worry, saying, 'What shall we eat?' or 'What shall we drink?' or 'What shall we wear?'….For your heavenly Father knows that you need these things. But seek first the kingdom of God and His righteousness, and all these things shall be added to you. Therefore do not worry about tomorrow, for tomorrow will worry about its own things."

Please, dear reader, do not think we are getting away from the subject of God's care. True, the Scripture stated above does speak of food, clothing, and even one's height; but notice that before Christ mentioned any of these, He spoke of "your life" (Mt.6:25). Does Jesus *care* about your spiritual needs? The answer is an unqualified yes! Earlier in this message some words of the hymn, *What a Friend We Have in Jesus*, were mentioned and quoted. There is another great hymn, *Does Jesus Care?*, which is appropriate for our topic because it is based on sound theology; thus it is true. It was written by a Methodist minister, Frank Graeff, in the early 20th century. Graeff went through some very difficult trials during his life. The period just before he wrote this song was one of great physical pain, doubt, and despondency. In our text—"casting all your care upon Him, for He cares for you"—he found great comfort. He studied and meditated on this verse of Scripture and others that expressed similar truths; then he wrote the words, with the assurance and resounding affirmation, in the chorus:

"O yes, He cares, I know He cares, His heart is touched with my grief;
When the days are weary, the long night dreary,
I know my Savior cares."

There are many verses in the Scriptures that point to the truth in 1 Pet. 5:7. We can—and should—take our burdens to Christ. And why does our text stress that we should do this? The answer is in 1 Pet. 5:7b itself—"because He cares for you." Jesus Christ knows our hearts and minds. He knows our hopes, concerns, joys, loves, dreams, fears, pains, and disappointments. He knows our needs, griefs, and weaknesses. He sees and cares for those who suffer day in and day out with affliction and sickness. Our text tells us to cast all of our "care upon Him, for He cares for you."

CHAPTER 3

IS YOUR HEART IN A FAR COUNTRY?

Scriptural Background: Luke 15:11-32

Text: Luke 15:31 "And he said to him, 'Son, you are always with me, and all that I have is yours.'"

In Luke 15:11-32 is found a commonplace story that frequently is commonplace today. Through the years it has been referred to as the story or parable of the prodigal son. However, I submit to you that it is more correct to label it "the parable of the two prodigal sons." This is carefully stressed by Jesus himself in Luke 15:25-32. Some biblical scholars are careful to point out that the older brother stayed at home, but his heart was in a far country. This heart was filled with greed, self-righteousness, and a total disregard of love or concern for the feelings of his father.

This should be a major concern for believers today. Why? Because as we worship, serve, and think of our relationship with our God; there is always a spiritual threat that we may think of ourselves too highly and take for granted our relationship with our heavenly Father and His nature.

Let me be more specific. In Deut.21:17 we find that when an inheritance was divided among a father's heirs, two-thirds of the estate was given to the oldest son. This was to be after the death of the father. The oldest son in this parable had already received his two-thirds of the estate—land, cattle, and other stock; yet, he was still living in his father's house. His self-righteousness blinded his relations with his father and his brother. Jesus was very careful to bring this to light in Luke 15:25-31.

The elder brother was free to use his inheritance any way he desired; but when the father with love and forgiveness wanted to restore the younger son and welcome him back into the home, the older prodigal paraded out his self-righteous record and threw a self-righteous fit. Our text shows how the father's heart and mind reacted: "And he said to him, 'Son, you are always with me, and all that I have is yours.'"

There is a real danger at times for Christians to elevate themselves and to rely on their past records and accomplishments. This is one of the major reasons all of us must examine ourselves and remember that our Heavenly Father and His Son alone are the foundations for forgiveness. All that we have and need for salvation, spiritual talents, our future, and any righteousness we have comes because the Father loves us and gave His Son for us.

This parable of the older brother can be used as a mirror for self-evaluation. I would suggest, however, that we ask God for forgiveness and the guidance of the Holy Spirit as we seek spiritual evaluation. It is then that we may better see our selfishness, judgmentalism, unkindness, and self-righteousness. The great danger, spiritually speaking, is that we may forget the great love and sacrifice Christ has given and made for us. As soon as we start believing that our lives and words show that we are impeccable Christians worthy of condemning others and are superior to them, it is then that we—in our hearts and minds—go to a far country.

It was Augustine who said: "A darkened heart is a far country, for it is not by our feet but by our affections that we leave Thee or return to Thee." Isaiah was a good man and a prophet, but when he "saw the Lord…high and lifted up…he said: 'Woe is me, for I am undone because I am a man of unclean lips and I dwell in the midst of a people of unclean lips'." In more recent history, Isaac Watts wrote:

"When I survey the wondrous cross,
On which the Prince of Glory died,
My richest gain I count but loss,
And pour contempt on all my pride."

It is in this attitude of repentance that we leave the far country of the heart and are once more reunited with our Father. We must avoid the poor belief that we possess the *right to judge and condemn others* who have failed, repented, and once more want to live for and with the Father. In Gal. 5:22 Paul, speaking of living in the Spirit, tells us that we are to show love, peace, long-suffering, kindness, and gentleness toward others.

Christians leave the far country of the heart when they realize that they are not sufficient in themselves and have no reason to glorify themselves—<u>save in the cross of Christ</u>. We have a Father who is beyond our full comprehension. Any righteousness we might have is imputed righteousness in Christ. The Holy Spirit still leads, guides, and reveals God to believers. God is able and willing to fill our greatest needs. Our attitudes and actions affect and influence others. They also affect us—for good or evil. There are commitments we must make and actions we must perform if we would honor our Heavenly Father. There are former ways of thinking and acting that must be put aside to stay out of a far country. We are to guard against thinking in terms of our greatness and more in terms of God's mercy and greatness.

A final indictment against the elder brother is very evident in this parable. He did not know his father; or, if he did, he had hardened his heart against his father's nature. Thus the younger brother showed more knowledge, love, and understanding of his father than did the older one. The older brother "missed the bus." He surely must have been a very unhappy and selfish person. If he had a family and friends, he must have been a very poor example for them.

There are three major differences between these two brothers that should be realized. <u>First, the younger one</u>, in Jesus' words, "came to himself" and realized his inadequacy. Moffat, in his translation, says: "But when he came to his senses," not only did he realize his incapability; in addition, he changed his feelings toward his father. He was aware that he had left a father and home that was worth far more than what his would-be friends' short-lived fun and spending—prodigal life—could provide. The elder prodigal in his spirit and inner motivation never really thought about this. He felt—if we may judge by his words and actions—that his impeccable, spotless record, character, and good behavior meant that he deserved to be treated as a superior person. Also he felt that his brother was not to be tolerated.

In the <u>second place, the elder prodigal never came to himself</u>. He never realized that this is God's world and he had a place in it. Furthermore, he seemed unaware of the fact that he needed to find that place and be of service to his father. It is a sign of spiritual and mental growth when a person learns that this is the Father's world; He makes the rules of life; and that one must—for a good and satisfying life—follow them. When we truly "come to our senses," it is then that we are beginning to draw near unto God, and He draws near to us. We as Christians know that this happens only when we let Christ be Lord of our lives. We also realize that this means repentance of sin and forgiveness through the Father's Son. In other words, we are saved to serve; not to drift in and out of fellowship and service to Him and His Kingdom.

Does God Care about You and Me?

<u>A third result</u> of coming to one's senses—which the older brother never realized—is that <u>life is for giving, not just for taking</u>. This means giving of one's self, talents, and possessions. We are not to view our existence as a chance to get all we can, but rather as what we can give to others. Someone has said a person comes to himself when he realizes that life is not for only getting and spending for one's self; but for giving to those who are in need, the work of the church, worthwhile causes in the community, educational institutions, and for providing for one's family. In essence, this means giving of one's self to God's kingdom and to others. The elder brother never showed or said anything that might indicate that these powerful forces were at work in his thoughts or life. His life can be a mirror for Christians today. It can show us our self-righteousness, judgmentalism, selfishness, pride, and vain glorification.

Now, in the previous pages we pointed out that the younger prodigal possessed three very important characteristics that the older brother did not have; nevertheless, we must remember that he *was* a prodigal. He was a prodigal, but he had attitudes and actions necessary for restored fellowship with his father. That made him redeemable, not hopeless. Let us review his case. Notice that he wanted whatever he was to get from his father's estate right then and there even though his father would have to make a great sacrifice. He did not ask his father's nor his brother's opinions. He wanted what he was to get of the estate regardless of all other's feelings.

Look again at Luke 15:12 which says: "...he (the father) divided to them (the two brothers) his <u>livelihood</u>." Here are two major negative and selfish attitudes—conceit and greed—and both sons possessed them. The younger prodigal <u>demanded</u> that his father give him his portion. Both sons were asking their father to divide to them his livelihood. You may now be thinking that the older brother did not make such demands, but—as pointed out earlier—really he did. As the oldest, he stood to profit the most; yet, instead of caring for and being concerned to stop the dividing of the estate, he was silent and gave no protest. By saying nothing, he was taking a position, one that contributed to the dividing of his father's livelihood. Christians today who take no stand against sin and evil living are in their silence taking a harmful position against our Heavenly Father's wishes and, indeed, sending poor signals to others—Christians or non-Christians. It is my belief that today believers are taking stands constantly for good or evil. It is something to think about; especially when we realize that others are being influenced by our actions and conversations.

Psychology—the study of the human mind—tells us a great deal about greed, conceit, and unthoughtfulness toward others. The younger brother had all of them, but he <u>came to his senses</u> in a far country when he <u>came to himself</u>. In other words, he started thinking about who he was and realized that as his <u>father's son</u> he was in the wrong place. He knew he should change his mind—repent—and go back to his father ready to serve even as a hired servant so long as he could be in his father's presence. He came to himself—he made a decision and then acted on that decision. He thought to himself: "I will arise and go to my father, and will say to him, 'Father, I have sinned…and am no longer worthy to be called your son. Make me like one of your hired servants.'" All of us in varying degrees have been in similar circumstances. Some of you reading this may be having such thoughts or in similar situations now. If so, let me suggest that there is only one way—and the only one needed: Confession of sin and the prayer, "Make me one of your servants."

The younger son had faith in his father and his nature. He <u>knew</u> that his father would forgive him, feed him, take him back, and put him to work and service. This <u>conviction</u> generated expectations of a better life, anticipation of fellowship with his father and family, and confidence that his father would be patient and show forgiveness and understanding to him. Our text says when "he came to himself," he made a life-saving decision: "I will arise and go to my father, and will say to him, 'Father, I have sinned…and I am no longer worthy to be called your son. Make me like one of your hired servants'."

Augustine was correct: "A darkened heart is a far country, for it is…by our affections that we leave Thee (God) or return to Thee." John Whittier had it right also when he wrote:

"Dear Lord and Father of mankind,
Forgive our foolish ways;
Re-clothe us in our rightful mind;
In purer lives Thy service find,
In deeper reverence, praise."

CHAPTER 4

BROKEN RELATIONSHIPS AND WHAT CAN BE DONE ABOUT THEM

SCRIPTURAL BACKGROUND: John 15:1-17

TEXT: John15:12 "This is My commandment, that you love one another as I have loved you."

How do you feel about your relationships with family, friends, co-workers, and your Lord? Strong, positive relationships are not just an accident; they do not just happen. They come about because of similar interests, feelings, and thoughtfulness. Good human and spiritual relationships are not perfunctory; that is to say, they are not brought about or performed merely as an uninteresting or routine duty. They are not superficial, devoid of interest, lacking in care or enthusiasm. Good positive relationships—mental or spiritual—develop because of patience, care, sustaining interest, and positive actions. For example, Jesus said: "By this all will know that you are My disciples, if you have love for one another" (John 13:35). John 15:12 states: "This is My commandment, that you love one another as I have loved you." John 15:9 gives further insights into Christ's teachings about love, relationships, and Christian living: "As the Father loved Me, I also have loved you; abide in My love."

This verse of Scripture shows that Christ felt it was essential for the disciples to realize that their devotion, love, and obedience for God, the Father, should be a deep, significant, association—a relationship, a connection, an involvement that would inspire "abiding love," trust, worship, and obedience.

In this message the writer would have you think of relationships in this manner: an association, a connection, an involvement, a love for God and others that is deep, significant, and important enough to inspire a positive relationship which leads to caring actions. As the text, John 15:12, states: "This is My commandment, that you love one another as I have loved you."

When a man and woman have true love for each other, they care for one another. This relationship can, and often does, lead to marriage, homemaking, and offspring. This type of relationship is not perfunctory; it is not merely a mundane or routine duty. It is more than superficial and indifferent; it is sincere and meaningful. That is the way it should be.

Brothers and sisters and their relatives should be connected by love and mutual interests; however, this is sometimes broken by envy, jealousy, hostile acts, and anger. In many cases, this comes about because of a lack of unselfish love or control of one's emotions and attitudes. Thus the relationship loses its caring concern for each other and becomes one of superficiality, indifference, and distrust. In other words, the positive emotional—love—attitude turns into a hostile, nonworking, angry relationship.

Jesus in His teachings set forth basic principles for good human and spiritual relationships in the home, community, and workplace; also in the church and His service. In the gospels are found the truths that should govern our relationships with God and with one another. The "sermon on the mount" is a classical example of what a Christian should strive to be *in relationship* to one's God and to others:

Becoming a blessed person (Mt. 5:1-1 2).

Having humility (Mt. 5:3).

Repentance and sorrow over sin (Mt. 5:4).

A gentle attitude toward God and one's fellowman (Mt. 5:5).

A righteous relationship with God—the righteousness of God in Christ Jesus (Mt. 5:6).

Showing mercy toward others and asking for mercy through Christ for one's self (Mt. 5:7).

A clean and pure heart in Christ (Mt. 5:8).

Striving for peace between others and yourself (Mt. 5:9). God's peace in one's own heart is a prerequisite for good human and spiritual relationships.

Living and standing for the righteousness of Christ Jesus (Mt. 5:10-11). His mercy, love, righteousness, and Christian relationships are to live in one's heart and be set forth in one's life.

Christians being a positive spiritual, God-preserving, and enriching influence in human society (Mt. 5:13).

The above statements were given by Christ Himself as guidelines for Christian living, loving, and witnessing in such a way that the right kind of spiritual relationships are born in our hearts and minds. John 15:12, the text, puts it in a very powerful way: "This is My commandment, that you love one another as I have loved you." This is not an oversimplification. It is a theme that runs throughout the New Testament and much of the Old Testament—such as the Ten Commandments, Psalms, and the Major and Minor Prophets. Indeed, one might well say that the overall concern of God's word, the Bible, deals with God's love for mankind and His concern that persons love one another and His Son—the Christ—and that His believers love the Lord their God with all their hearts, souls, and minds.

In many places in God's word one can find truths that deal with the importance, the sacredness, if you please, of abiding in close fellowship with God and Christian fellowship with others. John 15:1-10 tells us to abide in Him. Verses 4-5 give Christ's own words on these truths: "Abide in Me, and I in you. As the branch cannot bear fruit of itself, unless it abides in the vine, neither can you, unless you abide in Me. I am the vine, you are the branches. He who abides in Me, and I in him, bears much fruit; for without Me you can do nothing." Verses 6-10 continue to tell how crucial it is that we maintain unbroken fellowship with our Lord. Verse 11 crowns the previous verses by declaring—again in the words of Jesus: "These things I have spoken to you, that My joy may remain in you , and that your joy may be full." Our text then summarizes: "This is My commandment, that you love one another as I have loved you" (John 15:12).

From the above Christians can see it is the Savior's will that they indeed have a close, intense, and sacred relationship with Him and others. He also gives such believers His promises for answered prayer, fellowship, fruitful Christian service, glorification of the Father, and Christian joy. The hymn writer, E. A. Hoffman, put it this way:

"What a fellowship, what a joy divine,
Leaning on the everlasting arms.
What a blessedness, what a peace is mine,
Leaning on the everlasting arms."

Life often puts great pressure upon us; people misunderstand our attitudes, words, and actions. Selfishness, mistrust, and lack of patience rob us and others of spiritual energy, resolve, and Christian courage. This can result in broken relationships; however, there is help for those who would heed Christ's words: "If you abide in Me, and My words abide in you, you will ask what you desire, and it shall be done for you" (John 15:7). Note that Christ stressed in John 15:1-7 that just as a branch of a vine must abide in the vine, even so we must abide in Him. He put it this way: "Abide in Me, and I in you" (John 15:4a). This is the prerequisite that is required for a close and fruitful relationship of love and joy in Christ. It is also the requirement which must be met if John 15:7 is to be a reality in a person's prayer life and Christian service. If one is sincerely seeking to live our text, John 15:5: "This is my commandment, that you love one another as I have loved you," then he will have joy—His joy—and his witness will be fruitful. This is the ultimate way for healing broken relationships.

Yet we often are discouraged, lonely, and feel "de-powered," as one outstanding minister has said.[4] Confronting his own feelings of helplessness and confusion, Paul stated in Rom. 7:19: "For the good that I will to do, I do not do; but the evil I will not to do, that I practice." However, he did not let this inner struggle ruin his personal relationship with the Savior and with others.

Jesus used parables to show how broken relationships could come about between people and their Lord. One of the most outstanding is the parable of the Prodigal Son. After his father had given him his part of the inheritance, the younger son left their home and fellowship. In a "far" country he wasted his livelihood in prodigal living (Luke 15:13). Things got so bad for him that he was ready to eat the same food the swine were eating. Then the Prodigal started the process of true repentance. Luke 15:17-19 tells about it. He began evaluating his sad situation and "came to himself." Then he made a wise decision and acted on it. In his words: "I will arise and go to my father, and will say to him, 'Father, I have sinned…and I am no longer worthy to be called your son. Make me like one of your hired servants.'" The son returned to his father and was forgiven, and their relationship was restored. His father not only forgave him, but he welcomed him into the fellowship of his home.

The reception by the Prodigal's older brother was quite different. It was hostile and unforgiving which hurt the father and all concerned. That is another story; but it does show how selfishness, greed, and lack of concern for others can result in broken relationships not only with each other but also between persons and God, our heavenly Father. We are not to be guilty of the poor attitudes and criticism voiced by the elder brother. Above all, Christians—God's children—are to avoid the negative attitudes, cynicism, hard-heartedness, and inconsiderate manner of the elder brother when others repent and seek a new life with God through Jesus Christ. Rather one should rejoice when a fellow child of God turns away from a sinful life, repents, and seeks a closer relationship with the Lord and others. Again our text speaks to us: "This is My commandment, that you love one another as I have loved you" (Luke 15:12).

In the Old and New Testament are found many examples of those who hurt or destroyed their relationships with God and their fellowman. Some of them show how unbelief, bad attitudes, and hateful words caused good relationships to be broken. Others show how hurtful actions caused a loss of fellowship, good relationships, and positive actions. Some examples are briefly listed below:

> Gen. 3:6: Adam and Eve's unbelief of God's words spoken to them led to fear and to their fall from innocence and fellowship with God, the Father.
>
> Ex. 28:1: Aaron, who was made a high priest, later made the golden calf for the people to worship. This led to his exclusion from the Promised Land (Num. 20:12).
>
> 2 Sam. 13:29: Absalom murdered his brother, Amnon, because of his treachery toward his father and others; and was made

an exile from his home (2 Sam. 14:25).

Josh. 7:1: Achan's greed and disobedience brought about his death and the defeat of Israel at Ai.

2 Sam., Chapters 11-12 tell of David's lust and disobedience that led to adultery and murder.

1 Kings 12:4-19 describes Solomon's attitudes of unbelief, greed, and cynicism which led to the division of his kingdom and the worship of false gods (1 Kings 11:1-8).

John 18:25-29 relates how Peter, the disciple, lost his temper, became very angry, and denied the Lord Jesus in His hour of trial.

Mt. 27:3-5 states how Judas in his impatience, greed, and disbelief betrayed Jesus, which led to his suicide.

Acts 5:1-10 tells how Ananias and Sapphira's vanity, greed, envy, and hypocrisy led to their deaths.

Tim. 4:10 relates the story of Demas, who for some time served with Paul as a missionary; but abandoned his calling and Paul because of his love of the world and the things of the world.

The above are given as Biblical examples of serious broken relationships. Now let us think of Biblical truths that provide more suggestions for healing broken relationships in our lives. John 15:12, our text for this message, provides us with words from Jesus that certainly are worth studying and following: "This is My commandment, that you love one another as I have loved you." Not only this text, but the entire Chapter 15 of John's gospel highlights the importance of love—for God and for others. The book of John has as its major theme—love.

Several verses of Chapter 15 proclaim key ways for believers to avoid broken relationships and also how to rebuild those that have been damaged or broken. For example, Verse 9 says: "As the Father loved Me, I also have loved you; abide in My love." John 15:12 adds to this sound advice by Christ Himself: "This is My commandment, that you love one another as I have loved you." John 15:17 continues to stress love: "These things I command you, that you love one another."

The words of Jesus in John 15:1-14 deal with abiding in Him, love for God, prayer, and love for others. They move and inspire us, but they also give us pause; and we ask ourselves: *"How can we live up to these high standards?"* If we are honest with ourselves, we know that on our own it is impossible to do. Rom. 3:23 and many other Scripture verses remind us that "all have sinned and fall short of the glory of God." The words of Isaiah were true in his day and are surely true of us today: "All we like sheep have gone astray; we have turned, every one, to his own way; and the Lord has laid on Him the iniquity of us all" (Is. 53:6).

How then do the Scriptures point out what one should do when his relationship with God or man is broken? Rom. 10:9-10 gives the first step for a Christian or a non-Christian who seeks God's forgiveness. The first action is confession of sin: "For with the heart one believes unto righteousness, and with the mouth confession is made unto salvation." John, in his first letter, speaks to believers thus: "If we confess our sins, He is faithful and just to forgive us our sins and to cleanse us from all unrighteousness" (1 John 1:9).

The Prodigal Son's confession is often used as an example of a sincere and truthful confession (Luke 15:18). As stated earlier in this message, not only does one see true contrition but a resolve to get out of his transgressions and return to his father and the fellowship of his family.

The next step is repentance, which is being truly sorry enough to confess one's sins and take actions that lead away from sin and back to fellowship with God through Jesus Christ, the Savior and Lord. It involves the type of confession Thomas made in John 20:28 after the resurrection in which he said to Jesus: "My Lord and my God." After this repentance Thomas served his risen Lord, and there is no record of any unbelief or doubting.

The third step in restoring a broken relationship is action. Sincere confession and true repentance compels one to mental, spiritual, and physical action. The Prodigal Son came to himself; he thought through his hopeless situation and made a decision to return to his father, confess his sins, and serve his father. Thus the broken relationship was healed.

The Apostle Paul met Christ on the Damascus road and was converted and baptized—mental and spiritual activity—(Acts 9:3-18). After his conversion he preached in Damascus, then went into Arabia to think and pray. He returned to Damascus and preached (Gal. 1:17). After that, he became the courageous, militant, missionary apostle who served the Savior in preaching and writings, until his death.

Christ, however, is the one who is the perfect example for one's relationship with God, the Father—and also for relationships with others. In the home, with family, at work or in recreation, in good times or bad, in sickness, and even death, He "has set the example." Again, John 15:12, our text, states: "This is my commandment, that you love one another as I have loved you."

This message surely would not be complete without prayerfully considering John 15:26: "But when the Helper comes, whom I shall send to you from the Father, the Spirit of truth who proceeds from the Father, He will testify of me." Christians have a Helper—the Holy Spirit—to convict of sin, guide, intercede with the Father on their part, and provide the power for healing broken relationships with God and man.

CHAPTER 5

SPIRITUAL PROCRASTINATION—A MAJOR CAUSE OF MANY PROBLEMS IN CHRISTIAN GROWTH AND SERVICE

SCRIPTURAL BACKGROUND: Haggai 1:1-14

TEXT: Haggai 1:2b "This people says, 'The time has not come, the time that the Lord's house should be built.'"

Haggai, the prophet, is often referred to as "the prophet of the temple." It is believed that he was born during the 70 years of the Babylonian captivity and that he came to Jerusalem with Zerubbabel. Ezra 5:1 and 6:14 reveal that he was a friend and contemporary of the prophet, Zechariah. The text is Hag. 1:2b: "...the time has not come, the time that the Lord's house should be built."

The major theme of Haggai is serious and contains sharp rebukes to those who had returned from the captivity but were too busy with their everyday lives to rebuild God's house, the temple. On the other hand, he gives encouragement and key promises to those who decided to quit procrastinating and return to the task of rebuilding. Prior to Haggai's message, the returnees were selfishly preoccupied with their own work and building, beautifying, and enlarging their personal dwellings. Haggai told them that was the reason God was withholding His blessings from them (Hag. 1:3-6). Hag. 1:6 is concise and pointed in the summary of their situation:

"You have sown much, and bring in little;
You eat but do not have enough;
You drink, but you are not filled with drink;
You clothe yourselves, but no one is warm;
And he who earns wages, Earns wages to put into a bag with holes."

This writer feels that Verse 6 is saying: "You have put yourselves and your affairs before God and His work. He should be first in your lives." Building His temple would be the outward sign that God was to be given first place in their hearts, work, and lives. Haggai informed the people about what they should do concerning their miserable conditions. They were told to consider their ways—Verse 7. They did just that and God responded with blessings.

Surely, this Scripture speaks to us today. God's word and His work should be placed first in our lives. We should be very concerned to read, hear, consider, and truly give of our best to Him. He is worthy of our worship, praise, and service. Spiritual procrastination should not keep us from using our time, opportunities, and abilities in His service.

Procrastination is to put off intentionally the doing of something that should be done now. With many persons it is habitual, resulting in many missed worship services; lack of Bible study; forgetfulness; and neglect of prayer, daily devotions, and opportunities to witness and serve Jesus Christ.

For a Christian, personal procrastination often produces worry, feelings of guilt, sleepless nights, depression, and anxiety—just to mention a few of the emotional consequences. Such feelings are the very opposite of what God wants us to have. He wants us to feel and know His presence and peace. Christ wants us to have joy in our lives, faithful stewardship, and devoted service. This writer's study and personal experience indicate that procrastination robs a believer of the fruits of the Holy Spirit that Paul wrote about in Gal. 5:22-23: "...the fruit of the Spirit is love, joy, peace, longsuffering, kindness, goodness, faithfulness, gentleness, self-control."

In many cases in which persons are often or constantly putting off things that should be done; there are spiritual, psychological, or mental attitudes that shut out Christian fellowship, prayer, God's word, the Holy Spirit, and Christian service. Thus important tasks and services go undone, and the Christian finds himself drifting away from God's fellowship, useful Christian discipleship, spiritual growth, and opportunities. That is when he needs to repent, pray, and truly seek the Lord in His word, His presence, and service. A believer needs to understand that he can work out of spiritual procrastination and that God can supply the strength, guidance, and help for the inward struggle against the serious habit of putting off important actions, spiritual growth, and Christian usefulness.

The central purpose of this message is to consider some of the major spiritual, mental, and physical causes of procrastination that have been observed in study and work with Christians. As these causes are considered, some of the ways that spiritual procrastination can be overcome, according to the Bible, will be presented.

One of the most outstanding examples of spiritual procrastination so far as turning down an opportunity to accept Christ as Savior and Lord is found in Acts 24:25. Paul was before Felix, a powerful Roman ruler; and as he reasoned about righteousness, self-control, and the judgment to come, Felix was afraid, and answered, "Go away for now; when I have a convenient time I will call for you." In other words, Felix—in the words of our text—was saying: "The time has not come."

This writer has known many persons who in their homes, schools, and communities have heard the gospel but have never accepted Christ's invitation to "come unto me." They often have many reasons for their spiritual procrastination such as the following:

> I can't at this time because of my work schedule, etc.
> I don't really understand the Bible.
> I am too rushed with work, vacation planning, etc.
> I will think about it later.

But you know what they are really saying is found in our text: "The time has not come."

Jesus told a story once that many who have ignored John 3:16-17 should carefully read. It is found in Luke's gospel (14:16-24). We call it a parable today. It tells of a man who planned a large dinner and invited many to come; but, instead of responding to the invitation, they began to make excuses which could really be summarized in the words of Felix: "Go away for now; when I have a convenient time I will call for you" (Acts 24:25). Our text also speaks to this: "The time has not come, the time that the Lord's house should be built." The point in Jesus' parable is that the result of rejecting Christ as Savior—spiritual procrastination—has very serious consequences, and that God's invitation should have the highest priority in this life. In other words, what is the profit or gain if a person is rich, famous, popular, etc., but loses his own soul and life without Christ in this world and in eternity?

In the above paragraphs the very serious practice of putting off God's call for accepting His Son as Savior and Lord has been discussed. Some reasons for this type of spiritual procrastination were also set forth. However, our text, "The time has not come, the time that the Lord's house should be built," is not just referring to unbelievers. It is also speaking to God's chosen people; therefore, let us look at some of the major excuses for Christians' procrastination, many of which are the same ones that God's people in the Old Testament used. As we do so, keep in mind that God had delivered from the Babylonian captivity the people to whom Haggai was speaking and had commanded them to rebuild His house, the temple, that had fallen into ruins. May we, at the same time, remember that God has freed us from the captivity of sin and given us a new spiritual life in Christ Jesus.

One major cause of Christian procrastination is plainly given in our text: "The time has not come, the time that the Lord's house should be built." In other words, *procrastination* itself is a major cause of putting off what God's word tells us we should do and also the things God's Holy Spirit puts in our hearts and minds to do for Him and others. In Haggai's day the temple was more than just a building. It was supposed to be the center of worship. It was a place where God's honor dwelled (Ps. 26:8). To assemble and worship in God's house is a very sound way of life for us today.

To build and to worship in the temple was a command from God to His people in Haggai's day. In this Christian era we are to remember Paul's words about our bodies as a temple in 1 Cor. 3:16-17: "Do you not know that you are the temple of God and that the Spirit of God dwells in you? If anyone defiles the temple of God, God will destroy him. For the temple of God is holy, which temple you are." To this writer Paul is saying that our bodies must be kept pure, clean, and as dedicated to God and His service as we can possibly make them. This rules out abuse of the body in any form—overeating, the use of drugs, alcoholic abuse, sexual abuse, physical and mental abuse, and excessive and inordinate work. Also included are the sins that are labeled by Paul in Gal. 5:19-21a: "Now the works of the flesh are evident, which are: adultery, fornication, uncleanness, lewdness, idolatry, sorcery, hatred, contentions, jealousies, outbursts of wrath, selfish ambitions, dissensions, heresies, envy, murders, drunkenness, revelries, and the like."

By now you are probably thinking: "What does all this listing of sins have to do with spiritual and mental procrastination?" They have much to do with it. All of us have had to face and fight some or all of them; and the best way to deal with them is by thinking and doing the things that can cause the believer to resist them quickly:

>Repentance.
>
>Resistance to the practice of evil habits.
>
>The use of God's word.
>
>Prayer and dependence on God for the strength to overcome.
>
>Avoidance of those habits and persons who would keep one in the sin.
>
>Asking for God to lead, guide, and help every hour of every day.

Now some may say that the above suggestions are just a list of truisms; nevertheless, they are based on the Scriptures, and they indeed are true. When anyone feels that he can live above these truths, he will sooner or later find that he is putting off changes that must be made if he would have his life filled with God's spirit. In other words, if a Christian wants his life really to count for Christ and His work, he must get rid of sinful characteristics and habits; and this should be done quickly. Putting off repentance, needed mental changes, needed spiritual growth, and service for the Lord Jesus is spiritual and mental procrastination. It hurts the individual who is procrastinating; it interferes with the Lord's will and work in one's personal life; and it destroys one's witness to others.

As was pointed out above, our bodies are to be instruments of righteousness. Paul, led by the Holy Spirit, stated it so very well in Heb. 12:1-2a: "…since we are surrounded by so great a cloud of witnesses, let us lay aside every weight, and the sin which so easily ensnares us, and let us run with endurance the race that is set before us, looking unto Jesus, the author and finisher of our faith."

One of the leading causes of spiritual and mental procrastination is confusion and lack of organization in our lives. Yes, we live in a very *rushed* world. We do not want just the necessities of life, but much, much more; and we go from day to day trying to serve not only many people around us, but family and organizations as well. Much of life demands work and efforts from us. Our hurried lives, however, should not keep us from seeking God's help and presence—His Holy Spirit. We truly need to "be still and know that He is God." We need to remember Ps. 43:3a which says: "Oh, send out Your light and Your Truth! Let them lead me." And we need to pray constantly: "Hear, O Lord, and have mercy on me; Lord, be my helper!" (Ps. 30:10). Now you may be thinking: "You do not know the trials and burdens that I have to face." You are correct. I may know some, but God knows all of them. His word says we can cast all our burdens on Him because He cares for us. Thus when we find we are overwhelmed and confused, it is best to turn to our God and ask Him to help us organize our life, act purposefully, and deal effectively—and in a Christ-like way—with those who are around us. When we are so paralyzed by time limits, work, and duties that we cannot even see where to start; then it is that we must decide on priorities. It is the time we must decide to ask for God's presence, power, and help. God and you can develop a spiritual and physical plan of action. Above all, do not procrastinate. Paul said: "My God will supply your every need." If we avoid spiritual and mental procrastination, we can also deal with the emotional paralysis that results from the confused mind-set and the unaccomplished tasks that result from putting off what needs to be done today, this week, or this year. Christians, like many other people, often fail to realize that two great causes of our mental and spiritual procrastination are our failure to say "no" to demanding, overbearing persons and an inordinate (unreasonable) desire to please other people. Some jobs do demand too much of individuals; but confusion, lack of organization, and procrastination are often the problem.

Another cause of spiritual and mental procrastination is resentment of authority and people. This type of emotional factor builds anger, rebellion, resistance, and procrastination. Some believers sullenly come to resent others who make many "requests" and "demands." This can easily be the case of superiors who are "ordering" one around, and one has to do what they say. There are some Christians whose service and usefulness in God's kingdom work are compromised—hurt—because they have mental conflicts and attitudes toward those who are in authority. Individuals can do much harm to their Christian growth and witness by procrastinating and saying: "The time has not come."

Overcoming this type of procrastination involves three important actions. The first is *constant prayer*—for yourself—yes; and for the person or persons in authority. The second is to *talk with a fellow* Christian, pastor, Sunday School teacher, or prayer partner. Remember you and I alone are not enough to face all of life's problems; and we do not have to face them by ourselves. Many pastors and psychologists can give spiritual and mental help for Christians who resent authority. Please, however, do not gossip with others about your problems day after day; and do not constantly run to your "resource" person to bombard him or her. People cannot solve all of your problems; but if you seriously seek help from God and fellow believers, you will find it. A third action is *do not procrastinate*. Take time to pray, yes; to think, yes; but remember the longer you put off making a decision the more you will fall victim to mental and spiritual procrastination. Christians should wait on the Lord; but sooner or later we have to quit putting off what God sets before us as Christian duties and, indeed, opportunities to "take up" our crosses and follow Christ. We must not forever say: "The time has not come."

In conclusion, I would set forth the following recommendations on the basis of what I think the Scriptures have to say on procrastination and also what my research of written materials relates:

Ask God's help in your efforts to end the habit of constantly procrastinating. In other words, pray sincerely and repeatedly about it. God does hear and answer prayer.

Start small if you find that necessary. In other words, try to use the opportunities all around you to help others and serve your Lord. It may be just a word of encouragement, a phone call, an e-mail, a short note, a hospital visit, a prayer for a relative or friend—the point is, get started. Quit procrastinating.

When faced with large and challenging tasks, divide them—if possible—into smaller or manageable ones and do some of them to get started. "I can do all things through Christ who strengthens me" (Phil. 4:13).

Do not let a large opportunity overwhelm you. Progress—even small progress—builds spiritual and mental reassurance and peace of mind and encourages one to press on—press on for Christ. (See Phil. 3:13)

Pray and prepare to serve your Savior; but do not spend an inordinate amount of time getting ready. By this I mean it is better to go ahead and start than to procrastinate by trying to have the ideal situation arranged before you start to serve Christ. Jesus and the prophets never had everything just right before beginning their work.

Think, concentrate, pray for constant leadership, study your opportunities, pick your time for crucial decisions to be made and work to be accomplished. Use your ability, action, and Christian convictions—submitted to Him—to move you forward in the Master's service.

Work toward goals. People are goal oriented; and when spiritual goals and objectives are realized, there is inner satisfaction and success on which the Lord can give you faith, assurance, and confidence. Above all, do not say: "The time has not come."

CHAPTER 6

SPIRITUAL PROCRASTINATION PART 2

SCRIPTURAL BACKGROUND: Acts 24:22-25 and Haggai 1:1-13

TEXT: Hag. 1:2b "...the time has not come..."

Why another message on procrastination? Actually, this is a continuation of the first one. Procrastination—as set forth in the previous message—is a major cause of problems in spiritual growth and Christian service. It often keeps individuals from growing in knowledge and grace in the Savior, Jesus Christ. It sometimes makes mental and spiritual pygmies out of some who could have been intellectual and spiritual giants. This writer puts it that way because he has seen so many people cheat themselves out of business opportunities, valuable professional growth, spiritual blessings, and fruitful Christian service. In other words, procrastination is not to be taken lightly. It robs a person of peace of mind and Christian joy and prevents complete surrender to the Lord and His calling for faithfulness. It can keep a believer from ever knowing "it pays to serve Jesus."

Christian procrastination—as was stated in the previous chapter—is to put off intentionally the doing of something that should be done now.

It is failing to perform a service that a person knows should be done and he realizes, with the help of the Lord, he could do it. It may be as simple as visiting a sick or troubled friend, speaking a word of encouragement, providing help for the needy; or it may be something that requires much more time such as preparing to teach a Bible study or a Sunday School class. The point is that the Savior calls us to grow spiritually and to take up our crosses and follow Him. To this writer the taking up one's cross means the following:

> Growing in the love and knowledge of His word.
> Growing in His grace and mercy.
> Growing in faith and service to His church, our fellowman, and our families and loved ones.
> Growing in obedience and fellowship through the leadership of the Holy Spirit.

Acts 4:8a tells of Peter being filled with the Holy Spirit. After being commanded by the authorities in power to quit preaching and healing in the name of Jesus, he said in Acts 4:20: "For we cannot but speak the things which we have seen and heard." The early disciples—as well as many believers today—were like that. They had experienced the new birth, the coming of the Holy Spirit, and the power of the gospel to change lives; and they did not procrastinate. They took up their crosses and began serving. They knew they had a living Savior to serve and for whom to witness. It was not a matter of waiting for a more convenient season.

Now let us consider some of the other reasons—not discussed in the previous chapter—why believers procrastinate in Christian growth and service. As we do so, remember this is not meant to be presented as a guilt trip, but rather to help you and me to do some more thinking and meditating about the Christian life and Christian service. In other words, we should give thought as to how well we are living our beliefs and convictions. Wonderful things can happen when we take our beliefs very seriously and start living what we say and sing about as our convictions. The founder of the Salvation Army, William Booth, did just that. I remember a minister speaking about Booth in a Christmas sermon. Using Booth's own words, he said: "I got the poor of London on my heart…; on that day I made up my mind that God should have all of William Booth—all the adoration of my heart, all the power of my will, and all the influence of my life." Love of Christ, our Lord, calls all of us to be involved in His service; and to this writer this means finding an area or place of need—in our homes, churches, communities, and organizations.

Farmers and ranchers know they must keep weeds and grass out of their crops and pastures. Experienced Christians who have worked for their Lord and have lived very close to Him know that looking for a more convenient season or procrastinating when God and duty calls usually leads to unfaithfulness and lack of fellowship with the Master and Savior. Indifference, guilt feelings, worldly entanglements, and pursuit of worldly pleasures then take over in the heart, mind, and life of the person who says, "I will continue to procrastinate. I will tell myself 'the time has not come.' I will look and wait for a 'more convenient season.'"

Why do individuals do this? A major cause of procrastination is the lack of self confidence. Christians sometimes consistently procrastinate when they are faced with new opportunities or challenges with which they have had little or no experience. They fear they will not be very good at the new task or not be as highly competent in their work or actions. This feeling or lack of self-confidence can cause consistent procrastination, especially when the believer involved has very low self-confidence linked with an inferiority complex. What should a person do in such a situation? The answer, I believe, is to venture out in service—not trusting in his own ability or talents—but rather in faith asking God to bless his surrendered efforts to Him and His service. We need constantly to remember it is "'not by might, nor by power, but by my spirit,' says the Lord of Hosts."

This writer knows several believers who are very effective in responsible Christian service, but once were deep in lack of self-confidence. When they turned over their opportunities to serve to the Lord and asked for His guidance and help, they became very effective in their service. Remember the biblical example of Moses, who told the Lord he could not speak well, but he turned out to be a very accomplished speaker for God and the leadership of God's people. God's call to you may involve changing your priorities and your personal goals and objectives. Be that as it may, do not procrastinate because of fear or a lack of self-confidence. Rather tell the Lord how you feel about the situation, pray about it, and serve where you have the opportunity, asking Him for guidance, grace, and power. Do not say, "The time has not come," as the people in Haggai's day did; rather, say: "Here am I, Lord, send me." And as you do and serve, remember "every work for Jesus will be blessed; but He asks from everyone his best." Do not look for a more convenient season.

Spiritual procrastination that is caused by a lack of confidence can be a very distressing emotional burden, and it often places the Christian in a confused dilemma because it keeps feelings of doubt or incompetence alive in one's mind. At the same time, it causes the believer to avoid facing realistically one's limitations or capabilities. It is very true that none of us can do everything, but it is equally true that most of us can do something for our Lord and the work of His kingdom. Our challenge is to look daily about us and pray that God will not only show us what needs to be done, but that we will have the trust and faith to do it. The danger for many of us is that we start putting off decisions. We procrastinate;

and when we do, we live with constant reminders of what might have been accomplished for Christ—but were not. There are opportunities to serve all around us. "Look all around you; find someone in need; help somebody today." Do not put off what you can do. Remember the people Haggai was speaking to said: "The time has not come"; but God and Haggai said: "Let's start now."

God does call us over the rush, noisy demands, and opportunities of our "life's tempestuous sea." He does tell us today to be a living example of a believer and faithful, active servant of His. To follow His call when we find ourselves procrastinating because of a lack of faith and self-confidence, do the following:

Trust in Him to guide and supply the strength needed.

Continue to test your abilities under His guidance—many times, if necessary.

Set reasonable goals of service and test your talents to achieve them.

Talk with fellow Christians who show evidence that they are faithful in service and ask for their help.

Give up plans or objectives that are very unrealistic—until you and the Lord working in you have achieved smaller ones (work for worthy goals and service, however).

Get started.

Do keep trying to serve somewhere for Christ.

Remember the wonderful hymn, *Something for Jesus*. It was written by S. D. Phelps in the 19th century. The third stanza goes like this:

"Give me a faithful heart, like-ness to Thee,

That each departing day henceforth may see

Some work of love begun, some deed of kindness done;

Some wand'rer sought and won, Something for Thee."

> Do ask the Lord for help each day and seek daily opportunities for Christian fellowship and service.
>
> Do not let a lack of confidence, a pattern of inhibition, and procrastination prevent you from growing in Christ.

The people to whom Haggai spoke were telling him and God: "The time has not come, the time that the Lord's house should be built." Haggai told them they were wrong. He convinced them that the time was *now* to start rebuilding the temple. In Hag. 1:5 he told the people: "…thus says the Lord of hosts: 'Consider your ways'!" Verse 7 repeats these words; and Verse 8 shows why this message was so important: "'…bring wood and build the temple, that I may take pleasure in it and be glorified,' says the Lord." In Hag. 1:12b we find the reaction to his message: "…all the remnant of the people obeyed the voice of the Lord their God, and the words of Haggai the prophet, as the Lord their God had sent him; and the people feared the presence of the Lord." God's second message to the people was then delivered by Haggai in Verse 13: "Then Haggai…spoke the Lord's message to the people, saying, 'I am with you,' says the Lord." And Verse 14 continued the message: "The Lord stirred up the spirit of…all the remnant of the people; and they came and worked on the house of the Lord of hosts, their God." Hag. 2:19b gives us further insight as to that happened: "But from this day I will bless you."

In most areas of Christian service many have been timid beginners at one time or another. The term, *novice*, would be appropriate. To be afraid of new tasks of service for the Lord or to fear learning from one's mistakes may mean one has a sense of false pride. In other words, a person may be attempting to protect an image—an unreal image—of great confidence when he really may have no real reason to do so. Then when he does not do well, his confidence in himself is crushed—even though he has had no reason to feel he could do great things all along. God can truly move in powerful and mysterious ways, but only when the individual is completely surrendered to the Lord's will, and the cause is clearly for Christ and His kingdom's work. The key to keep in mind—to this writer—is to drop the unrealistic pretense. Ask God for guidance and help as to what course of action you should pursue. Above all, do not say: "I can't do anything for the Lord." Do not procrastinate. Do not say, in the words of our text: "The time has not come." Pray that God will help you to be more open to His will and to teach you to be more flexible and less the victim of self-imposed procrastination.

There is another reaction or force that is a type of self-sabotage. It often leads to procrastination. Many sincere Christians develop very mixed emotions, attitudes, and self-doubts about opportunities, spiritual challenges, or changes that might possibly occur if they were to accomplish certain goals or objectives for their Lord. They then put off opportunities for service in Christ's kingdom. Often these Christians later condemn themselves for their lack of action for the Savior. Also they are very verbal at times about their behavior, saying: *"If only* I had done so and so for the church or for Christ." Seldom, however, do they see that really they are ruining their Christian service and their power to "serve the Lord with gladness."

Sometimes they are afraid that they would be expected to assume more responsibilities and new roles as a surrendered servant of the Lord. Thus they let their opportunities to be effective Christian ambassadors pass. They procrastinate. In the words of our text, they say: "The time has not come." They sing: "Every work for Jesus will be blessed," and the hymn is true; but they will not commit themselves. They are "almost persuaded," but they refuse to become an active soldier of the cross. Such believers can be faithful in attendance at the church services. They are often good workers in business and the service industries. They may be faithful supporters of the church financially, which is very important; but God needs teachers, witnesses, church officers, and many others who are willing not only to sing: "I will do what you want me to do, dear Lord; I will be what you want me to be"; but will also serve as God leads and opportunities present themselves. In other words, He needs people who will work for Him now; who will not put off their service; who will not say, in the words of our text: "The time has not come."

There is one other cause of spiritual and mental procrastination which is sometimes referred to as the pleasure priority or force. The term refers to persons—in this case, believers—who put fun, pleasure, recreation, harmful habits, enjoyment, and idleness ahead of spiritual growth, self sacrifice, and Christian service. When there must be a choice between a recreational experience such as sports events, hobbies, days and nights of television, or some other worldly pleasurable opportunity; they choose it over worship or service for Christ-like causes. This is not to say an individual should not have some recreation, hobbies, rest, or relaxation; frankly, I believe they should. These factors should not dominate their lives, however. These activities should not keep them from helping others, serving the Lord, and being actively involved with the activities of the church. In the words of our text they should not over and over keep saying: "The time has not come."

Unfortunately, for many, "putting off" or procrastination has become a way of life. Thus churches have to beg members to teach, hold offices, visit the sick, help those in need, and minister in other ways. Procrastination can become such a pervasive habit that an individual may accept it as normal Christian behavior. It is surely not in keeping with New Testament discipleship. Procrastination can interfere, disrupt, and prevent individuals from growing in spiritual knowledge, joy, peace, and service.

What should the concerned believer do about procrastination? Here are some suggestions which I think are based on common sense and biblical truths. As you read them, think of our text which Haggai used to move God's people in his day when they were "putting off" what God had *asked* them to do: "This people says, 'The time has not come, the time that the Lord's house should be built.'"

> Try to identify the reason or cause that makes you put off what you know you should be doing for your spiritual welfare and for God's service.
>
> Confess your sins and ask God to help you overcome your procrastination (this suggestion and the first one are essential). Repentance must come first; then there must be prayer for strength, resolve, and God's presence (Acts 1:8).
>
> Be patient, but ask the Holy Spirit to help you act purposefully (1 John 2:28).
>
> Set goals that, with God's help, you think you can accomplish. Try to so order your days that you truly can apply yourself to grow in knowledge and Christian service (John 12:26).
>
> Be *willing* to pay the price, make the sacrifice, and quit procrastinating. This, in most cases, will not be easy if one has fallen into the habit of constant procrastination; for example, putting off helping or serving others, prayer, and Bible study; and seeking worldly pleasures first, neglecting family, etc. Christ paid the price for our redemption; He now intercedes for us at God's throne. He promised in Mt. 28:20b to be with us always. Thus we should not say: "The time has not come" for me to think, pray, set spiritual goals, or act for His kingdom. We should not say: "I am waiting for a more convenient season or time."
>
> Arrange your work and life-style so that critical spiritual

decisions and tasks are accomplished. Mental conflict and confusion will haunt or dog you if you do not. You can defeat procrastination with God's help and thus feel better about your spiritual self. You will also experience God's presence and fellowship in a much more real and reassuring manner!

When opportunities for spiritual growth and discipleship present themselves, do not ignore them. Do not procrastinate nor—in the words of our text—say: "The time has not come."

Serve the Lord with gladness and joy. Arrange your time tables or schedules so that you make room for Christ and His calling. Learn to trust and obey—yes, it is something a person has to learn. Do not say that the time has not come.

CHAPTER 7

CAN YOU VISUALIZE THIS?

SCRIPTURAL BACKGROUND: Heb. 10:16-25, 11:1-6, and 12:1-6

TEXT: Heb. 12:2a "Looking unto Jesus, the author and finisher of our faith."

The book of Hebrews is full of tremendous spiritual truths. Outstanding biblical scholars have written volumes of sermons based on this book alone. In this message the writer wants to share some of the thoughts that have come to him as a result of his study of Chapters 10, 11, and 12 of Hebrews. In these chapters the author, who most authorities say is Paul, was concerned that the people to whom he was writing understood that Christ's coming, ministry, message, death, and resurrection had brought about a far superior dispensation than that of the Old Testament prophets. Indeed, the entire book of Hebrews speaks to the fact that Christ is the fulfillment of the Law and the Prophets—which He was and is. It also brings out that Christ is far more superior in the following ways:

    He is a much better revelation of God and His word (Heb. 1:1-2).

He gives to believers a much better hope (Heb. 7:19b).

He is a better—and a divine—High Priest (Heb. 7:22-28).

He sets forth a better covenant (Heb. 8:6).

He sets forth better promises based on that covenant (Heb. 8:6b).

He is a far better sacrifice for sin (Heb. 9:22-24).

He gives to believers better possessions—everlasting life, fellowship now and through eternity, and a home with Him in Heaven (Heb. 10:34b-36).

He gives a better country—Heaven (Heb. 11:16).

He gives a better resurrection (Heb. 11:35b).

However, Heb. 12:2a: "Looking unto Jesus the author and finisher of our faith," has been selected for the text of this message.

What does Paul mean by the expression, looking unto Jesus? He means that we are to visualize Christ as our Lord and Master and that, with our spiritual vision, we are to look daily to Him for *strength, guidance,* and *wisdom.* In Eph. 1:18 we are told that we have spiritual eyes; and, indeed, we do. God's word, the Bible, constantly speaks of persons who had visions and insights to His messages and works. Today we also can see God—in His word, in the lives of others, in world events, and in our everyday and spiritual lives. Thus we conclude that "looking unto Jesus, the author and finisher of our faith" means just that; that He is to be our role model, the one to whom we look for victorious, dynamic, fruitful Christian living. It is with our minds and spirits that we are to be looking unto Jesus. Then as we see—even though it is only in part—we can better visualize what He would have us to be and do.

Reading specialists tell us that good readers can visualize what they are reading. In other words, they are not just calling words. If they are reading about cars, they see cars. If their reading deals with trees and leaves in spring or fall, they visualize these things. With our minds we think, remember, set spiritual goals and objectives, and we can live our lives in unselfish service for God and others.

Many times in the field of psychology we read that the thoughts and pictures we have in our minds determine what we are, do, and become. The young athlete practices hard as he pictures himself as a successful, mature member of a team. The would-be-successful business person pictures himself as a success and works toward that end. In Heb. 12:1-2 Paul said that there are those all around us who view what we do and say. In light of this fact he then stated: "Let us lay aside every weight, and sin which so easily ensnares us, and let us run with endurance the race that is set before us, *looking unto Jesus.*"

To this writer "looking unto Jesus" involves that which has already been stated; but it means more. It surely must include creating mental pictures of biblical truths for ourselves and for others to witness in our lives, and it further involves developing guidelines of service for Christ. These guidelines or Christian convictions are to keep us "looking unto Jesus." They are to be spiritual handrails; or, as Mrs. C. H. Morris wrote in one of her great hymns: "I've anchored my soul in the haven of rest." The visual images we place in our minds become our memories, thoughts, convictions, attitudes, and codes of Christian conduct or lack of it. The Psalmist wrote in Ps. 119:105: "Your word is a lamp to my feet, and a light to my path."

The mental images we place in our minds through reading, viewing, listening, speaking, and living make us what we are. If we fill our minds with God's word and spiritual truths and then work to keep these convictions as guidelines for our living, we avoid many evil forces and can better serve our Lord. In other words, we learn to "trust and obey." The visual images—pictures, if you please—serve as motivation for the type of living we do and the service we render or do not perform. The alcoholic pictures his drinks, goes after them, and pays the price for the images he creates in his foggy mind. The drug addict does the same. The devoted, faithful Christian studies God's word, uses his mind to visualize what needs to be done in his own life, home, community, and world. He then does that which God's Holy Spirit leads him to do, and the service he performs is controlled by his "looking unto Jesus." In my office and home I have pictures of my family and loved ones. These pictures remind me of who I am and to whom I should be loyal. Filling one's mind with God's word, worshiping Christ as Savior and Lord, constantly thanking Him for His grace and mercy, doing for family, loved ones, and others is—to this writer—"looking unto Jesus." This I believe is what Christ meant when He said: "Take up your cross and follow me."

When I was in the third grade, I had a wonderful Sunday School teacher named Mrs. McDuffie. She had already reared her children and was now helping to rear her grandchildren. She was really good at working with little ones. One Sunday just before Christmas she asked the class to close their eyes and pretend they were present the night that Jesus was born. Until this day I can remember some of the questions she asked us to think about and imagine: "Can you see the baby Jesus in the manger? Can you see some of the animals present? Can you see some of the people who crowded the Inn? Can you see Mary and Joseph? Can you see the shepherds who came to worship Jesus?" In other words, she was asking us to visualize the scene and time of the birth of our Savior and Lord, the Christ. That one Sunday School lesson and the pictures that came to me as our teacher asked the class to imagine—to visualize—the nativity scene and those involved in it—still live in my memory.

While I was in college, a Bible teacher asked my class to "picture in your minds events and teachings associated with the life and ministry of Jesus." On one occasion in a prayer he asked that his and the class' eyes might be opened to the great teachings of the Christ. He went on to pray that we, as a result of our spiritual visualizing, might come to a greater realization of God's greatness, His love, and the importance of the gift of His Son. When he had ended his prayer, he called to our attention Scripture verses from the prophets Jeremiah, Isaiah, and Micah that foretold the coming of Christ. He closed the class by briefly discussing John 3:16.

When Jesus spoke these words, He was talking to Nicodemus, a rich Jewish leader, "a member of the sect of the Pharisees" (John 3:1 TLB). Nicodemus knew what Jesus was saying about the necessity of a new birth. A spiritual rebirth was something that was required of a Gentile who would accept the Jewish teachings and laws and thus become a Jewish proselyte. But the two words Nicodemus used in speaking of being born again conveyed a different meaning from those used by Christ. Nicodemus was using the term in a horizontal religious sense; whereas Jesus was stressing the absolute need of a complete change of heart—a rebirth of the soul. This was a vertical spiritual heart change that resulted in far more than a shift from any Gentile religion to Judaism. It involved an acceptance of Christ as the promised Messiah and a belief in Him as the Savior of the world. This demanded an act of faith and the reception of Christ as the "Lamb of God" who takes away the sins of the world. Can you visualize the conversation that Jesus had with Nicodemus? Hopefully, you can and hopefully, with the aid of the Holy Spirit, you and I can get a renewed vision of the importance of Christ's coming for mankind, the forgiveness of our sins, and the blessedness of being a child of the King through the New Birth in our hearts and minds.

This message is being written at a point in history when our country is in great economic, political, social, civic, moral, and spiritual trouble. Many leaders of great companies are being investigated and taken to court. Some outstanding political leaders in positions of great power—local, state, and national—are not measuring up to the trust people have placed in them. Social and legal agencies are burdened with tremendous problems, numbers of cases to solve, and thousands of persons they are expected to serve. Schools are overcrowded, and good teachers are in short supply. The sick and suffering overcrowd hospitals and nursing facilities. Spiritual leaders in some of the major denominations and in television and radio ministries have failed their followers. How is the Christian to respond to all of this?

First, let us realize that none of us have all the answers, and in many situations we may be part of the problem. Visualize your past life and see people, events, actions, and work that you know were factors and influences which were the direct result of God's Spirit working in your heart and life. Then thank God that He has used you in His kingdom's work. Ask Jesus Christ, your Savior and Lord, to cleanse your mind, heart, and life so that from this moment on you truly will be "living for Jesus a life that is true." Pray that, by humbleness, willingness, and obedience, you may become more like our Savior and Lord. Then as we think of His love, humility, and zeal to do His Father's will and to serve mankind, may we truly feel and say as the hymn writer, Frank A. Breck, did many years ago when he wrote:

"Look all around you, find someone in need; Help somebody today. Tho' it be little—a neighborly deed—Help somebody today."

As you try to visualize—mentally and spiritually—think of these words composed by another great spiritual giant, Clarence H. Scott: "Open my eyes, that I may see Glimpses of truth you have for me."

When we think of the many things God has done for us and the many blessings He has bestowed upon us; may we, like the apostle Paul, be ready and willing to say with great resolve and commitment: "...since we are surrounded by so great a cloud of witnesses, let us lay aside every weight, and the sin which so easily ensnares us, and let us run with endurance the race that is set before us, looking unto Jesus, the author and finisher of our faith, who for the joy that was set before Him endured

Does God Care about You and Me?

the cross, despising the shame, and has sat down at the right hand of the throne of God" (Heb. 12:1-2). Paul continued this exhortation for faith, Godliness, and service in Heb. 12:3: "For consider Him who endured such hostility from sinners against Himself, lest you become weary and discouraged in your souls." In other words, in this chapter of Hebrews he was saying:

> Visualize Christ as your inspiring example—"He was obedient even unto death" (Heb. 12:2-3).
>
> Visualize Christ—His faithfulness, endurance, love, patience, joy, suffering, and death on the cross for those who will believe in Him (Heb. 12:1-3).
>
> Visualize—or as Paul said in Verse 3—consider what you can be and do for your Lord and for others.
>
> Visualize—goals and objectives for your spiritual life.

Think about the four statements listed above. Visualize spiritual goals and objectives for your life. Many people who have resolved their financial debts have discovered that it was necessary to set goals and objectives for the wise use of their money and credit cards if they were to become financially secure. Many very intelligent and many not so smart have been unwilling to set financial goals and objectives. This is also true in the mental, physical, and spiritual realms of life. If a person does not use his mental ability to reason, think, study, and learn; he becomes stunted mentally. The individual who has little or no concern for his physical condition courts the risk of poor health, sickness, and premature death.

In our spiritual life we remain "babes in Christ" unless we visualize and set goals and objectives for spiritual growth and development. We can also become a spiritual stumbling block to others. In the hymn, "Make Me a Channel of Blessings," Harper G. Smith wrote about this truth, and he brought out that Christians can be a barrier and a hindrance if their lives are not free from known sin. They can also become very ineffective disciples of the risen Lord if they are taken up by the cares and concerns of this world and have no goals and objectives for moral and spiritual growth.

By the term, spiritual goals, the writer means that Christians need large spiritual objectives such as a life led by the Holy Spirit, a strong desire to be a living testimony for Christ, great assurance and faith in the risen Savior, deep biblical convictions; and a manifestation of these convictions in daily living, in words, and deeds; an inward peace, and a keen desire to help others to know Jesus Christ, our Savior and Lord.

By the term, spiritual objectives, this writer also means doing the necessary things that lead to spiritual growth. To be specific, set spiritual objectives in Bible study and readings. Fill your mind with God's word. Have as a major objective to hide His word in your heart. Make His holy word truly a light for your pathway in this journey toward eternity. Set objectives in witnessing to your loved ones, colleagues, and those you see on a daily or frequent basis. Have a daily and meaningful prayer life; and, above all, do as Paul did—strive for the high calling of God in Christ Jesus.

There are other areas that involve objectives for spiritual maturity; for example, consecration such as the early disciples had. In Acts 4:13 we find these words: "Now when they saw the boldness of Peter and John and perceived that they were uneducated and untrained men, they marveled, and they realized that they had been with Jesus."

Verses 17 and 18 of Chapter 4 tell us that the powerful rulers of the Jews called Peter and John "and commanded them not to speak at all nor teach in the name of Jesus. But Peter and John answered and said to them, 'Whether it is right in the sight of God to listen to you more than to God, you judge. For we cannot but speak the things which we have seen and heard'" (Acts 4:19-20). Can you visualize this? Peter and John had had their personal experience with the risen Savior, and it had transformed them from weak and fearful men to powerful ones who had received the Holy Spirit and were willing to risk all—even their very lives—for their Lord and Savior, Jesus Christ. We need such a vision for our day and our lives.

Can we have such a vision? Can we have such a transformation in our lives? Can we—Christians in the 21st century—receive the power of "God's presence" in the form of the Holy Spirit? The answer to these questions is a very sound, "Yes, we can." The promises, power, and presence God gave to the early disciples are available to believers today. Christ promised never to leave us alone. The power of God's Holy Spirit has not diminished; therefore, we can be obedient, faithful, and useful for our Lord now. This should be our major goal in life. Jesus said in Mt. 6:33: "But seek first the kingdom of God and His righteousness, and all these things shall be added to you." In Mt. 7:24 He said: "Therefore whoever hears these saying of Mine, and does them, I will liken him to a wise man who built his house (life) on the rock...and it did not fall, for it was founded on the rock." The Christian's hope, faith, and trust are "built on Jesus' blood and righteousness"; and for our strength, guidance, spiritual vision, and eternal hope, we look to Him. The believer in this 21st century is to "Let your light so shine before men, that they may see your good works and glorify your Father in heaven" (Mt. 5:16).

In conclusion, this writer is restating four statements listed earlier:

> Visualize Christ as your example. Try to do this every day; or as Paul said in Heb. 12:2a: "Looking unto Jesus, the author and finisher of our faith...."
>
> Visualize His faithfulness, patience, love, and death for all who will believe in Him. Having done this, remember Phil. 4:19: "My God shall supply all your need according to His riches

in glory."

Visualize what needs to be done in your life—pray, study, seek His guidance; do what you see should be accomplished for Christ and His kingdom. In John 14:12 Jesus said: "He who believes in Me, the works that I do he will do also; and greater works than these he will do, because I go to My Father."

Set goals and objectives—in Bible study, worship, praise, service, and faithfulness. In 2 Tim. 2:15 we find these words: "Be diligent to present yourself approved to God, a worker who does not need to be ashamed, rightly dividing the word of truth." And in 2 Pet. 3:18 God's word says: "But grow in the grace and knowledge of our Lord and Savior, Jesus Christ. To Him be the glory both now and forever." We grow and develop as Christians as we read and study His word, be of service to others, look unto Jesus for spiritual direction and guidance, and keep ourselves "free from known" sin.

Lastly, refer to Phil. 4:8-9: "Finally, brethren, whatever things are true, whatever things are noble, whatever things are just, whatever things are pure, whatever things are lovely, whatever things are of good report, if there is any virtue and if there is anything praiseworthy—meditate on these things. The things which you learned and received and heard and saw in me, these do, and the God of peace will be with you." In our hearts and minds may each new day find us "Looking unto Jesus, the author and finisher of our faith."

CHAPTER 8

NO ROOM FOR THE SAVIOR?

A Christmas Message for Every Day

SCRIPTURE: Luke 2:1-20

TEXT: Luke 2:7b "There was no room for them in the inn."

There are many texts in the Bible—both the Old and New Testament—which give keen insight to important truths and the situations in which they were first written or spoken. Some of them are especially helpful when persons ask for God's Spirit and presence in their study. Approached in this manner, they give believers opportunities to learn practical, timely, timeless, and extremely important truths for Christian living. Such knowledge is needed for one to know Christ better, serve Him more faithfully, and witness more effectively. True and lasting fellowship with the Savior comes only as we make room for Him and His word daily in our lives. Believing that these statements are true, one has to wonder why the words of Luke 2:7b are as true of today's world as they were of the one into which Jesus was born. "There was no room for them—Mary, Joseph, and the Christ child—in the inn."

These words—no room for them—are a sad commentary on the residents of Bethlehem at that time. They were religious; they had Abraham as their "father" which made them proud. Josiah, Micah, and other prophets had foretold the coming of a king, Messiah, Savior, who would be called Jesus because He would save His people from their sins. But when Christ was born, there was "no room" for Him in the inn. Indeed, in the days of His earthly ministry most of His own people rejected Him, His message, and the major reason for His coming—to seek and to save those who were lost.

The inn keeper and his guests were under great pressure. Their country was occupied by the hard and cruel forces of Rome, which caused them to live in anxiety. In fact, the true reason why most of them were in Bethlehem was to register and pay taxes to the Roman rulers. Poverty, worry, and fear probably drained their souls as they waited in Bethlehem to pay tribute to Caesar Augustus. It is still difficult to believe that they would not make room for Joseph and Mary, a young woman who was about to give birth to her first child. This is especially true since within the last year there had been so many miracles associated with this woman and promise of the Christ child. Consider the following which were widely proclaimed in Jerusalem and all Israel:

Zachariah and his vision and sudden inability to speak.

The birth of John after Elizabeth's childbearing years had passed, and the prophecy of Zachariah.

Gabriel's enunciation to Mary, the Angel's foretelling of the name and lordship of the Messiah, Mary's visit with Elizabeth, and the birth of John the Baptist.

Zachariah's ability to speak restored and his prophecy concerning the Christ child.

The point this writer would have you grasp from the above is that there were many reasons why the people in Israel at that time should have shown more kindness and concern for Mary, Joseph, and their unborn child. They were religious, the children of the covenant, the ones who had been looking for the coming of a messiah.

Why, then, did they not show concern for this couple and their unborn child in light of the above listed miracles? There were probably many reasons. The Romans were forcing these proud citizens of Israel to pay taxes to Caesar. Their country was occupied and controlled by enemy soldiers and high ranking government officials who cared little or nothing for the Israelites. Still one has to wonder why the inn keeper and his customers could not find room in their hearts for better treatment and kindness for the expectant Mary and Joseph.

Think again of the text, Luke 2:7b: "There was no room for them in the inn." One might well say, as many outstanding ministers have said—Jesus was at that moment "the excluded Redeemer." Those present surely must have known about Mary's condition. Some must have known that they had been sent to a stable for the night where Mary had brought forth her first-born child and that He was lying in a manger, a feed trough for animals. Thus Jesus, the Savior and Lord, was born into such a world—a world lost in darkness of sin; filled by people—religious people—who had no room for their redeemer, no compassion or concern for the Christ child or His parents. Even a casual reading of the gospels will reveal that this same state of affairs—this rejection, this hardness of heart and mind, this sense of selfishness, this lack of sympathy and concern controlled the people of His day even until His death and resurrection. "There was no room for (Jesus) in the inn."

To a great extent this is the situation today. Many individuals are controlled by concerns for making a living and for finding diversions in recreation, entertainment, and the pursuit of secular happiness. In their minds and hearts there is no room for a living Savior. It is only fair, however, to acknowledge that there were sincere believers in Israel who were looking for the coming of a Messiah just as today there are people who live full lives with many interests, who work hard to support their families; but Christ Jesus is the Lord of their lives. This is shown in their choice of worship over lazy indifference or half-hearted devotion. It is manifested in their heartfelt prayers and concern for their loved ones, relatives, friends, fellow workers, and those who do not believe in Christ as Lord and Savior. In other words, they make room for the worship and witness of a living redeemer. This should be a major objective in life.

Christ would have every person make room for Him in their hearts. He calls individuals to know Him better and to experience His love, mercy, and presence in a stronger, more personal way. He seeks to have them open the doors of their hearts, minds, and lives. His word still stands: "Behold, I stand at the door and knock. If anyone hears My voice and opens the door, I will come in to him and dine with him, and he with Me" (Rev. 3:20).

Today Christians and non-Christians have great forces pulling them in many directions and away from the "Blessed Redeemer"—Jesus Christ. Christians know from their own experiences that it is often hard to live a spiritually fulfilling life for Christ. Yet, this is exactly what the Savior wants individuals to do, and it should be their major goal. Jesus would have all persons come to Him, and He would also have all believers to abide in His presence. As was stated above, He stands at the door of our hearts seeking entrance. This surely means many things; but a study of the New Testament clearly states that it means fellowship, peace, the Holy Spirit and Its power, and our highest honor as children of the eternal God. Sin, however, breaks that fellowship, destroys Godly peace, drives away the power of the Holy Spirit, and undermines our faith and trust in the only begotten Son of God. It also destroys our usefulness as witnesses and workers in God's kingdom. Why do Christians and non-believers allow this to happen?

Does God Care about You and Me?

The Savior, Jesus, the Son of God, tries to draw us away from selfish desires and to Himself instead. He would have us come away from any influences which would charm and chain us to the exclusion of faithful discipleship. This is the reason why it is worth our time to think about the *forces* that attempt to exclude the Christian from usefulness in His service and enslavement to harmful habits, ways of thinking, and actions that reject and exclude our Lord from our hearts, minds, and, in short, our daily work and living. So again, let us consider Luke 2:7b: "There was no room for them in the inn." As we do, may we keep uppermost in our thinking the biblical truth that if we draw near to Him—Jesus, the Savior—He will draw near to us. At all times we need to realize that He would have us know Him in a better, deeper way; and that truly, as Paul stated in Eph. 4:1, Christians are to walk worthy of His calling. James put it this way: "But be doers of the word, and not hearers only, deceiving yourselves" (James 1:22).

Why is Christ the Lord often excluded from our hearts, minds, and lives? Two major reasons are *indifference* and *unconcern*. These two are linked together because they are often inseparably working against sinner and saint. Today's world makes tremendous demands upon us. We spend much of our time striving to survive. Advertisers constantly try to get our time and money by persuading us to buy their brand of goods and machines that we need plus those we do not need. They attempt to make us seek after whatever they say we should have; thus we spend much on that which provides little satisfaction for the present or the future.

This writer would not set himself up as a judge or know-it-all; but rather he would simply state what he and humble Christians, ministers, and teachers see and hear every week. Indifference and unconcern motivate many to live as the priest and Levite in the story of the good Samaritan (Luke 10:30-35). When they see the need to give to others or to help the sick and needy, they pass by on the other side of the road.

E. Dale Davis

Some have often heard and read the words of Christ as given in Mt. 25:34-40; but they are still indifferent. At times in the past the story of the coming of the Prince of Peace may have meant much to them. Others in their youth accepted Christ as Lord and Savior, but now their hearts are flooded with other interests. Fellowship and service for the Savior have been pushed aside by an "I could care less" attitude and the false idea that they can manage their personal lives without the eternal Lord of Life. To them indifference and unconcern have replaced knowing Christ as a friend who knows and understands all about them, and who seeks to enter into their hearts, interests, and daily living; in short, truly to be their *Savior* and *Lord*.

Luke 2:7b states: "There was no room for them in the inn." An indifferent and unconcerned person cannot experience His grace, forgiveness, and help in the trials, difficulties, challenges, and perplexities of life that sooner or later all must face. In other words, if unconcern and indifference fill one's mind, little room is left for Jesus to be Lord of that life.

What about our minds, hearts, and lives? Does Jesus find room in them or does *unconcern* and *indifference* crowd Him out of our innermost thoughts and often out of our lives? As we think of His birth, life, and sacrifice, may we not have the attitude of the innkeeper and his guests. Let us put aside unconcern, selfishness, and indifference and make room for the Son of God, the Savior of the world.

Another reason that many people have no room for the Lord who seeks to fill their lives is that often they are *preoccupied* with the secular world and its demands. This was true of those at Bethlehem when Christ was born, and it can be true of persons today. This writer is not suggesting that we have no concern for family, friends, making a living, and so forth—not at all; but rather that in our living we should make room for Him as we worship, work, and go about the various activities of each day. This would seem to be a reasonable task, especially considering the precious promises of God and our Lord and Savior. Some of these promises are listed below:

> Never to leave us alone (Mt. 28:20).
>
> To supply our every need (Luke 12:29-31, Mt. 6:8, Phil. 4:19, Heb. 4:16).
>
> To prepare a place of eternal rest and peace with Him in a home in heaven (John 14:1-3).
>
> To hear our prayers when they are in keeping with His will (Mt. 6:6-13).
>
> To make anyone His child when one comes to Him in faith and belief (Mt. 11:28, John 7:37, John 10:10).
>
> To forgive our sins when we repent and ask for forgiveness in His name (Mt. 6:12-15 and Luke 11:4).

It is this writer's belief that the innkeeper and his guests would have made room for Mary, Joseph, and the Christ Child if they had been rich or persons of power; however, they were quite the opposite. In their preoccupation with other things, these individuals had no desire to help provide shelter and assistance to such lowly citizens. Being absorbed with the material, social, or recreational often fills our minds and lives to the extent that there is no room for the Savior who wants to be and should be the Lord of our lives. Numerous times this writer has found himself so concerned with the things of this world that Luke 2:7b, our text, "there was no room..." definitely applied to him. Why is this true of so many people today? In the pursuit of the material, recreational, educational, and whatever else, why do we not realize that if we have no room for our Savior and Lord, we are at best "babes in Christ" and spiritual failures; and, if unbelievers, lost and moving toward eternal failure? These are truths straight from the Bible, truths not invented by man.

There are other reasons that cause us to be so preoccupied with the things of this world that even believers have little or "no room for" Christ the Lord. These stand out and are worthy of special prayer, thought, and action. Not attempting to overcome these factors by our own strength, we must, instead, look to Jesus. Paul stated it well in Heb. 12:1-2a: "Therefore…since we are surrounded by so great a cloud of witnesses, let us lay aside every weight, and the sin which so easily ensnares us, and let us run with endurance the race that is set before us, looking unto Jesus, the author and finisher of our faith."

An additional reason is one about which many others have written; that is, the fact that the world can and often does make us its slave. The world wants to shape and dominate our thoughts, attitudes, habits, work, social, and recreational life. Is it any wonder that John warned the people of his day not to love the world or the things of the world (1 John 2:15)? Today Jesus calls us through the words of His book, the Bible; but the demands of the world preoccupy people's minds and chain them, even their perception, goals, thoughts, and attitudes. The word, *world*, in this discussion means those material forces, thoughts, and actions which crowd out belief, faith, worship, service, love, and loyalty to Christ. Paul referred to them as the things of this world, and so they are. When persons let these things control their hearts and minds, they are indeed enslaved and prisoners.

By His death and suffering for our sins on the cross Jesus has provided a path for repentance, forgiveness, and fellowship with Him and our heavenly Father. Thus when our self-seeking for things and useless pleasures of this world decreases, God's peace, strength, and fellowship with us increase. God is always seeking to help us rise above the littleness of worldly things and concerns. When we put Him first in our thinking and living, He can, and will, enable us to do great things for Him and for others. You say: "I have tried to put Christ on the throne in my heart, to make Him Lord of my life, to put Him first and in the center of my thoughts and actions; but I have been unable to overcome the unchristian forces, my self-seeking, and my own weaknesses." This is an honest statement that in truth has applied to many of us. What then is the answer and solution to the situation? In all sincerity, let me say that it is often difficult to know the answer; however, Christ has provided it for us by His sacrifice and in His living word. God's plan is for us to believe and trust Him fully for salvation, power to overcome sinful weaknesses, and strength to endure and serve.

There are other forces that often crowd out Christ; and, in the words of our text, make "no room" for Jesus (Luke 2:7b). It may be one or more of the following:

> The *inordinate* or *unreasonable* desire to be socially popular with others.
>
> The *controlling* desire to be entertained, watch sports, or engage in other time-consuming activities.
>
> The *enslavement* or *inordinate seeking* of academic pursuits or intellectual honors.
>
> The *unreasonable* and *blind seeking* of unneeded wealth and power.
>
> The *passion* to pursue hobbies and interests at the expense of worship, Christian service, and family life.

The list could be extended on and on, but that is not the point. *Simply put, believers must not let any one or more interests* fill and control their lives to the *exclusion* of Christ, His Lordship, and service. A Christian's goal in life should be commitment and service to the Savior. He must be the center of our being. Other things—such as those listed above—may be perfectly harmless when engaged in with reason and thought. The danger is we may let such things become a controlling factor, an idol which we serve and follow, to the exclusion of the Son of the living God; the one who loved us and gave Himself for our sins. Jesus put it this way in Luke 16:13: "No servant can serve two masters; for either he will hate the one and love the other, or else he will be loyal to the one and despise the other. You cannot serve God and mammon." The hymn writer had it right when he wrote: "Nothing between my soul and my Savior...Keep the way clear; Let nothing between."

Another *powerful force* that can cause the words of our text to be true in our lives is the fact that many of us let the past failures, secret sins, and previous experiences keep us from providing room for Jesus. Hanging on to these makes us prisoners in the present and distrustful of the future. Some seem to cherish secret sins of the past and use them as an excuse for not finding room for Christ. Unconfessed or secret sins and hardness of heart can ruin our attitudes, service, devotion, and fellowship with other believers and our Lord. These sins should be confessed and forsaken. We can then make room for the Savior.

In Phil. 3:13-14 Paul stated: "...one thing I do, forgetting those things which are behind and reaching forward to those things which are ahead, I press toward the goal for the prize of the upward call of God in Christ Jesus." Paul made room for Jesus, his Savior and Lord. May we do likewise. Let it not be said of us: There was "no room" for Him in our hearts, minds, and lives.

CHAPTER 9

PRE-CHRISTMAS THOUGHTS

SCRIPTURAL BACKGROUND: Mt. 5:43-48

TEXT: Mt. 5:46 (TLB) "If you love only those who love you, what good is that? Even scoundrels do that much."

It was the seventh of December, and I was not feeling too great. I was behind in my Christmas shopping; I needed to get some Christmas cards; my yard was full of dead leaves—most of them from my neighbors' oak and poplar trees; and worst of all, it was December seventh. Since 1941 this had always been a bad day for me. Yes, in my heart I had forgiven the Japanese for the atrocious attack on Pearl Harbor; but the day still brings back bad memories of the terrible four years of war. They were not only terrible years for those in the Armed Forces, but also for many on farms, in factories, and in the shipyards across the nation. But Mt. 5:46 leaves no room for hate or hardness of heart. It simply, yet boldly, states that you and I are to love not only those who love us, but also those who do not love us.

This verse brings to remembrance what Christmas is all about. It is wonderful to have friends who care for us, help us, open doors in life for us, and comfort us in sickness and in times of sadness; but Christmas reminds me that I am to love, care for, and help those who may or may not care for me, or know me, or even love me. For you see, fellow believers, Christ died for you and me while we were yet sinners; yes, even before we were conceived in the womb. Mt. 5:43-44 in *The Living Bible* reads: "There is a saying, 'Love your friends and hate your enemies.' But I say: 'Love your enemies! Pray for those who persecute you'!" And consider just a part of the next verse—the first sentence of Verse 45: "In that way you will be acting as true sons of your Father in heaven."

Truly, we should care for, love, and pray for Christian friends as we approach Christmas. We should also be very thankful for them. We should pray for the peace of God that passes understanding to come into their hearts and into our own; yet, we should pray and work for peace in the hearts of others. We should especially be concerned for those who are in need of spiritual, material, or mental help. We should do what we can, and we can surely pray for others with petitions that are more than mechanical repetitions. Our prayers should be sincere, from the depth of our spiritual beings.

At this time of the year it is cold in most of the United States. For many there is a shortage of basic needs. There are many homeless people—in the cities and in small towns. It is indeed a time to remember Jesus' words: "It is better to give than to receive." Winston Churchill once wrote: "We make a living by what we get, but we make a life by what we give."

Now, as I begin to feel better about Christmas, I remember again that winter of 1941. My mother and father had very little to give, but during that year they had been able to share with neighbors in need some food we had grown on the small farm on which we—with the help of a merciful God—existed.

But I must not give the wrong impression. I used the expression, existed, and in one sense that is the proper one; yet, it is true only in a materialistic sense. My parents never possessed very much of this world's goods, but they taught all of us eight children how to work. Yes, we had to work so we could live and go to school. They were determined that we would go to church and to school. In school we were not only to do what the teachers said to do, we were also to respect them and to learn from them. But there was more than this involved in my parents' teachings. They taught us the joy and wonder of Christmas and what it was all about. To them it was more than a time of buying and exchanging presents. It was a time to contemplate the miraculous—the birth of the Son of God, the Prince of Peace, the Savior of the world.

I remember on one December morning just before dawn my father and I returned to the house after feeding the livestock. My mother was standing on the back porch. She said, "Look up at all those lights." The morning stars seemed so low that they appeared to be just above the trees. When we went inside for breakfast, her only comment as she looked at me was, "Quite a sermon, don't you think?" She and my father had peace in their hearts. At this time of the year truly we need to pray that He might fill our hearts with love and peace, and that we might then be a blessing to others. A good place to start is a thoughtful reading of our text: "If you love only those who love you, what good is that?"

As one great spiritual writer has pointed out, an outstanding, Christ-filled, productive Christian life is the "accumulation of grace-filled days."[5] In other words, the past is gone; yesterday is spent for good or bad. Christmas past will not return, but we have today and, God willing, tomorrow. So what is the point? Before and after this Christmas let us live for Christ and for others. Remember Jesus Himself said: "He that would find his life must lose it,"—yes, lose it in service. Jesus still says to us today: "Take up your cross and follow Me." Surely, that means doing for the Savior what we can where we are.

So since our yesterdays are gone; our futures are not here; we should make use of today. We must be *faithful* and *obedient* to the Savior, the Lord Jesus Christ, *today*. If we serve Him faithfully each day, truly "it will surprise you what the Lord has done" with our time and abilities over a period of a week, a month, a year, a lifetime. As Ogilvie has pointed out, the recovering alcoholic struggling to get rid of his overpowering habit makes a daily commitment to be sober for one day at a time.[6] So we must strive—one day at a time—to be pure, "without and within," and do what we can for others and for our Lord and Savior, Jesus Christ. The things we want to accomplish for our Lord's kingdom and for others can be done by God's grace and power under the leadership of the Holy Spirit. Our text exhorts us to love others; not just those who love us.

As time propels us toward this new Christmas, I get encouragement from two sentences given to me by my secretary, Mrs. Cartwright: "Yesterday is already a dream and tomorrow is only a vision; but today, well-lived, makes every yesterday a dream of happiness and every tomorrow a vision of hope and love" (author unknown). She later gave me a copy of a poem by the great Bishop Samuel Wilberforce. I say it is a poem; it really is a great prayer. Read it slowly:

> Lord, for tomorrow and its needs I do not pray;
> Keep me, my God, from stain of sin, just for today.
> Let me both diligently *work* and duly *pray*,
> Let me be *kind* in word and *deed*, just for today.
> Help me to mortify my flesh, just for today;
> Let me no wrong or idle word unthinking say;
> Set Thou a seal upon my lips, just for today.
> Let me in season, Lord, be grave, in season gay,
> Let me be *faithful* to Thy grace, just for today.

In a very real way the decision to love others is up to us. Jesus said: "Lo, I am with you always—even to the end of the world." "I will never ever forsake you." "My grace is sufficient for you." "Ask and you will receive, seek and you will find; knock and it will be open to you." "I stand at the door and knock; if any man (person) will open the door, I will come in and have fellowship with him." Before this Christmas, let us do a little soul searching, and remember our text: "If you love only those who love you, what good is that? Even scoundrels do that much."

Jesus was God made human flesh: Born as a small baby, grew to manhood, was tempted as we are—yet without sin, suffered and died on the cross for the sins of the world, was buried but rose from the dead, was seen by His disciples and many others after His resurrection, ascended to His heavenly Father, and now rules on high. He sent the Holy Spirit to lead, guide, and comfort; and all of this is only part of what God has done for us. In other words, we owe Him our all. In the book of Deuteronomy God spoke to His people and urged them to make the right choice: "For this is the commandment which I command you today....Choose life" (Deut. 30:11, 19). Choosing life today entails looking to God as the people of Israel were told to do; but it also means for Christians to look to, believe in, and live for a Savior who came to earth that they might have eternal life. Jesus taught that we should love one another. Our text states that we are to love—not only those who love us—but "even scoundrels."

In Ps. 91:11 God said that He will give His angels charge of us—to guard us in all our ways. Think of it! Think of the wonder of it. At that first Christmas God sent His angels to announce the Savior's birth. Think of it! Today God still says that He will give His angels charge of us to guard us in all our ways. Why? This surely must mean letting our lives show we love Him and love others.

In Is. 41:10 we read: "Fear not, for I am with you; be not dismayed for I am your God. I will strengthen you. Yes, I will help you, I will uphold you with My righteous right hand." Earnestly believing God's word, let us consider Heb. 4:16: "Let us therefore come boldly to the throne of grace, that we may obtain mercy and find grace to help us in time of need." Think of this promise. God's grace forgives our sins, cleanses us from unrighteousness, and promises us help in our times of need. It is stated in another way as a prayer of David in Ps. 30:10, and it is one we might well pray today: "Hear, O Lord, and have mercy on me; Lord, be my helper." Again in Ps. 28:7: "The Lord is my strength and my shield, my heart trusted in Him, and I am helped…."

But we are not to receive grace and help just to be selfish. We are to love, worship, and serve—serve with joy. Consider Mt. 11:20; Jesus is speaking: "Take My yoke upon you, and learn from Me, for I am gentle and lowly in heart, and you will find rest for your souls."

SUMMARY AND CONCLUSION

Christmas is a time for wonder—worship—giving, but also for service—and helping others. So what does it mean to Christian believers? To this writer it means the following:

   A. Christmas means the promised *Messiah has come*. Is. 9:6 reads: "For unto us a Child is born, Unto us a Son is given; And the government will be upon His shoulder. And His name will be called Wonderful, Counselor, Mighty God, Everlasting Father, Prince of Peace." Mic. 5:2, 5: "But you, Bethlehem Ephrathah, Though you are little among the thousands of Judah, Yet out of you shall come forth to Me The One to be Ruler in Israel, Whose goings forth are from of old, From everlasting…. And this One shall be peace."

   Mal. 3:1 is another one of many found in the Old Testament: "'Behold, I send My messenger, And he will prepare the way before Me. And the Lord, Whom you seek, Will suddenly come to His temple, Even the Messenger of The covenant, In whom you delight. Behold, He is coming,' Says the Lord of Hosts."

In the New Testament His birth was foretold to Joseph as is recorded in Mt. 1:19-23, Mark 1:7-8, Luke 1:26-31, John 1:6-18. John said of Jesus: "Behold! The Lamb of God who takes away the sin of the world!" (John 1:29b).

B. Christmas means that God has sent His Son to be the *Savior* of the world. John 3:16-17 tells us: "For God so loved the world that He gave His only begotten Son, that whoever believes in Him should not perish but have everlasting life. For God did not send His Son into the world to condemn the world, but that the world through Him might be saved."

C. Christmas means that our Savior is *always with us*. Mt. 28:20b tells us: "And lo, I am with you always, even to the end of the age." Acts 1:8a gives more assurance of God's presence: "But you shall receive power when the Holy Spirit has come upon you." John 17:26b supports this teaching: "…that the love with which You loved Me *may be in them*, and I in them." Our text supports this.

D. Christmas and Easter mean that we *serve a living Savior* who, indeed, is in the world today. And our Savior has said this about those who will work for Him today and in any age: "Assuredly, I say to you, inasmuch as you did it to one of the least of these My brethren, you did it to Me" (Mt. 25:40b).

E. Christmas means that we have *eternal life*. John 3:15 says that "whoever believes in Him should not perish but have eternal life." John 3:16-17 confirms this.

F. Christmas means God's *peace* for believers. Jesus said: "Peace I leave with you, My peace I give to you; not as the world gives do I give to you. Let not your heart be troubled, neither let it be afraid." Paul, writing to the Ephesians, said: "Grace to you and peace from God our Father and the Lord Jesus Christ" (Eph. 1:2). Luke 1:79b tells us that Jesus came "to guide our feet into the way of peace." In Luke 2:14 he continued by saying: "Glory to God in the highest, and on earth peace, good will toward men!" The great preacher and hymn writer, Charles Wesley, stated it well when he wrote: "*Peace* on earth, and mercy mild; God and sinner *reconciled*."

G. Christmas also means *joy* to Christians. Isaac Watts wrote in his hymn, *Joy to the World*: "Joy to the world, the Lord has come! Let earth receive her king." John quoted Jesus in his gospel, saying: "Ask, and you will receive, that your joy may be full" (John 16:24). In John 16:22b Jesus, speaking of His death and resurrection, told His disciples: "You now have sorrow; but I will see you again and your heart will rejoice, and your joy no one will take from you." Peter wrote to believers in his day, saying: "Now you do not see Him, yet believing, you rejoice with joy inexpressible and full of glory" (1 Pet. 1:8b). Paul, in many of his writings, stressed peace and joy; for example, in Gal. 5:22 he spoke of joy and peace as two of the fruits of the Holy Spirit.

Nahum Tate in his Christmas hymn, *While Shepherds Watched their Flocks*," wrote: "Glad tiding of great joy I bring to you and all mankind… All glory be to God on high, and to the earth be peace." Paul said in Phil. 4:7: "The peace of God, which surpasses all understanding, will guard your hearts and minds through Christ Jesus." Paul's world was full of trouble and conflict. So is our world; yet God's word promises peace and joy to Christians. Henry W. Longfellow said it well when he wrote: "God is not dead, nor doth He sleep; The wrong shall fail, the right prevail, With peace on earth, good will to men."

Sometimes it is hard to love even those who love us. Families often have clashes of goals, habits, money management, and personalities. Some love their own relatives like a spare tire is used—only when an emergency occurs. Church members are at times argumentive, have hard feelings, and an unforgiving spirit toward fellow believers. Jesus taught that we are to love one another as God loves us. Our text, in Jesus' words, asks: "If you love only those who love you, what good is that? Even scoundrels do that much." "Let us love one another for love is of God." That is what Christmas is all about.

CHAPTER 10

OVERCOMING ONE'S MENTAL, SPIRITUAL, AND PHYSICAL ENVIRONMENT

SCRIPTURAL BACKGROUND: Hebrews 11:32-40 and 12:1-3

TEXT: Heb. 12:2a "Looking unto Jesus, the author and finisher of our faith."

Christian character is composed or made up of mental, spiritual, and physical factors. An individual can analyze his Christian character by prayer, spiritual and mental reflection, meditation, Bible study, and letting the Holy Spirit search every aspect of one's mind, heart, and physical activity. Christian character is the product—the result—of those factors all around that has made a person—for good or evil—what he is.

Individuals can be defeated or strengthened by the way they respond to their mental, spiritual, and physical environment. This can be a series of constructive or destructive thoughts or actions that over a period of time make them what they are. By choosing, seeking, and holding to the forces around them; people either succeed or fail by these choices and how they respond to their environment. A negative environment can be overcome, or one can let it master him.

With the help of the Lord an individual can overcome a harmful environment—as Paul did when a prisoner in Rome; or when surrounded by a favorable one, he can use it for greater opportunities for spiritual growth and service. The reaction to factors all around him can make all the difference. Today those factors usually consist of, but are not limited to, immediate family, relatives, friends, fellow workers, fellow believers, community, television, radio, newspapers, and magazines. It can be quite a challenge to be able to avoid letting environment or any surrounding factors overpower him. On the other hand, the person who overcomes in life can do so because one, or a collection, of influences or factors inspired or influenced him not only to overcome overwhelming odds, but also to go on to greatness in material, educational, and spiritual achievements.

The Bible—in the Old and New Testament—gives many examples of individuals failing when they should have succeeded and numerous instances in which they failed when they could—with the Lord's help—have been victorious in their personal lives and in service to others:

> Adam and Eve were placed in a garden—an environment—where there was everything they needed and no sin. God, however, asked one thing of them—not to eat of the tree of good and evil. They disobeyed His commandment and were driven out of the garden.
>
> Cain failed to give a proper sacrifice to God, and God did not respect his offering as He did Abel's. God told Cain what he should do about this; but he refused to follow His instructions. The result of this was jealousy of Abel, which led to Cain's killing his brother (Gen. 4:3-10).
>
> Other examples are Lot, a worldly-minded believer, who chose Sodom as a place to live (Gen. 13:12); Saul who ruined himself and his kingdom with his jealousy of David and

other sins (1 Sam. 31:4); Solomon, who at first was a man of wisdom, but in later life followed the evil advice of his foreign wives and restored the worship of false gods in Jerusalem (1 Kings 11:6-10); Samson—the weak—strong man who let his lust bring about his downfall and death.

In the New Testament there are many who had wealth, knowledge, and positions that should have assured them of victory over their surroundings; however, they let elements in their environment destroy and shape them toward evil and uselessness. Ananias and Sapphira pretended to be giving more than they really were and thus—in Peter's words—lied to Peter and the Holy Spirit (Acts 5:1-10). Demas was Paul's associate on the mission field at first, but later he forsook—abandoned—him. 2 Tim. 4:10 tells why: "…Demas has forsaken me, having loved this present world and has departed for Thessalonica." There are many others who could be listed.

On the other hand, there are many who can be given as examples of those who, in spite of great odds, overcame many difficulties and became powerful individuals in character and in service and usefulness for their Lord. Consider just a few of them:

Abel believed God and followed His instructions.

Noah, the ark-builder, believed God, warned the people of his day, and for 120 years worked to construct the ark (Gen. 6-8, 7:12). The Scriptures describe him as a person who "walked with God" (Gen. 6:9).

Abraham, the spiritual pilgrim, whose name means *father of a multitude*, believed God and obeyed Him. Heb. 11:8-10: "By faith Abraham obeyed when he was called to go out to the place which he would receive as an inheritance…. By faith he dwelt in the land of promise.

Joseph was sold into Egypt. He received divine revelations; and he remembered to honor God, accepted providential circumstances, sought and received divine guidance and help, resisted temptations, was faithful in business dealings, and was a Godly influence to others (Gen., Chapters 30-50).

Daniel is another shining example. There are many similarities between his and Joseph's experiences as youths and adults. Both were captives when they were young. Each one seems to have been a gifted individual, and both worked for kings who did not believe in the true God, Jehovah. They were faithful to their beliefs and teachings. He had to suffer for his convictions, but he did overcome adversities.

Other outstanding examples are Moses, Aaron, Joshua, Gideon, the eleven faithful disciples, Paul, Barnabas, Cornelius, Joseph—the husband of Mary, Luke, Philip, Stephen, Timothy, Silas, and Zacharias—the father of John the Baptist.

Heb. 11:32-35 states: "The time would fail me to tell" of many others "who through faith subdued kingdoms, worked righteousness, obtained promises, stopped the mouths of lions, quenched the violence of fire, escaped the edge of the sword, out of weakness were made strong, became valiant in battle, turned to flight the armies of the aliens.... Others were tortured, not accepting deliverance, that they might obtain a better resurrection."

Think with this writer about some of the many women who had the faith and courage to live and stand fast for their divine beliefs and convictions. Think also of the ways God used them as a result of their faithfulness. Here are some found in the Old Testament:

Bathsheba, the mother of Solomon (2 Sam. 11:3).

Deborah, a prophetess who judged Israel (Judges 4:5).

Esther, who helped the people of Israel avoid great calamity.

Hannah, who was the ideal mother (1 Sam. 1:20).

Huldah, who was a prophetess (2 Kings 22:14).

Miriam, an older sister of Moses, who saved him when he was a baby (Ex. 2:4).

Naomi, whose name means a pleasant person (Ruth 1:2, 2:1).

Rachel, the wife of Jacob and mother of Joseph and Benjamin (Gen. 30:1-25).

The following are some women found in the New Testament:

Anna, whose name means grace, was a prophetess (Luke 2:36) who prophesied in a world controlled by Romans and hardhearted Jewish leaders.

Dorcas, who was brought from death back to life (Acts 9:36), was a benevolent woman of Joppa who rose above the evil society around her.

Elizabeth, whose name means oath of God, was the mother of John the Baptist (Luke 1:5). She believed God and overcame her surroundings.

Eunice was the mother of Timothy (Acts 16:1). She was praised by Paul (2 Tim. 1:5).

Martha was the sister of Lazarus, who was raised from the dead by Jesus (Luke 10:40). She was known for her spiritual knowledge (John 11:24.

Mary, the mother of Jesus—our Savior and Lord (Luke 1-32).

Mary, a faithful Roman Christian according to Rom. 16:6. Paul recognized her as a faithful worker for Christ.

All of the above overcame great forces of evil and prejudices that they might indeed master—with the help of their Lord—the strong traditions and pagan forces all about them. Our text tells us how we can overcome: "Looking unto Jesus." Yet, we are human and often very weak in our faith and Christian service. In too many cases we condone, approve of, and practice life styles, habits, and ways of thinking that reflect a life that portrays a person who appears to *blend* in with a secular, materialistic society that cares little for the spiritual values and faithfulness to one's Lord.

In stating the above, the writer is not trying to be judge and jury toward others. His efforts here are not to condemn, but rather to point out that many of us need to pay much greater attention to practicing what we have been taught and have accepted as sound biblical doctrine. It is good for us to be thankfully aware that there are many, many believers who have deep convictions about their Christian faith and are living them in private and before others day by day. In most cases, they are people who are humble in spirit, do resist evil, do overcome the lack of spiritual concern of others and harmful life styles and habits of the secular world. They are able to practice and witness for the Living Lord. They are very much aware of the fact that "we are surrounded by so great a cloud of witnesses"; but they also know that to overcome evil in this or any society, they must heed and follow Heb. 12:1-2a: "…let us lay aside every weight, and the sin which so easily ensnares us, and let us run with endurance the race that is set before us, *looking unto Jesus*, the author and finisher of our faith…."

The following discussion presents *some* of the more promising ways that believers in Christ Jesus as Savior and Lord can overcome their environment.

1. We are to lay aside "every weight, and the sin which so easily ensnares us, and let us run with endurance the race that is set before us,

looking unto Jesus" (Heb. 12:1). It is through *looking unto Jesus* as the Lord of our lives that we—with the help of the Holy Spirit—can overcome sin and any force that would separate us from the one who seeks to be the Lord of our lives. He can *daily* supply the strength and power needed to overcome evil in our lives if we are *looking unto Him*.

Christ is the basic prerequisite for a victorious Christian life and fruitful Christian service. Many individuals who are not Christians have done much good for man and the secular world about us; however, to make one's life free from the enslaving power of sin and to fulfill the highest potential for God and others, it is necessary to *look unto Jesus* as Savior and Lord.

The recommendation for an individual to find victorious living by looking unto Jesus may seem to be too simple for many people who sincerely want to overcome evil in their lives and render Christian service. Let me assure you it is not simple. In fact, it is a major spiritual challenge. Paul tells us to "lay aside the sin which so easily ensnares us and to look unto Jesus."

Remember the story of David and Goliath. Goliath and the Philistines were taunting King Saul and his army (1 Sam. 17:6). Remember also that David wanted to intervene, but his own brothers made fun of him and told him to go home. Saul himself told David he could not fight this giant; but David pointed out to Saul how God in the past had helped him defend his father's sheep against a bear and a lion. David gave the credit to God for these past achievements and assured Saul that God would deliver him out of the hands of Goliath (1 Sam. 17:36). Before David killed the giant, however, he proclaimed that he was going out to meet him in the name of the God "of the armies of Israel" (1 Sam. 17:45b).

This is not just a simple story to tell to children. There are valuable truths in it that speak to us today. For example, are there *great giant problems* in your life that need to be faced and solved? If so, would you trust God and ask Him to help you face them? He is still the same God. He is able to deliver you if you face these "giant" problems in His name, praying that the request is within His will.

We, as people of faith, must see beyond the Goliaths before and around us. Our text tells us that we are to live the Christian life "looking unto Jesus." God will provide help in overcoming the evils that are in our surroundings. We must be persistent in our faith and efforts, and we must constantly ask for the leadership and power of God in those efforts.

Saul and his army were looking at the threatening giant and the Philistine army. They expected hopeless defeat continually day after day because they were not looking or asking for strength and victory. On the other hand, David saw the possibility of victory because he had learned to trust God and look to Him for victory. We are to be *looking unto Jesus* as David looked to God. This is the way we are able to overcome corrupt forces in our environment.

The persons of faith set forth in the Scriptures are worthy of our attention and consideration. God's word applies to us today just as it did to those named and written about in His word. Let us continue to think about our text, Heb. 12:1-2a. How do we "lay aside every weight and the sin which so easily ensnares us"; and how do we "run with endurance the race that is set before us, looking unto Jesus…"? One very specific way is *looking unto Jesus* as Savior and Lord of our lives.

2. Another suggestion is the *turning away, leaving behind*, or forgetting those sins of the past that would keep us from growing in our faith and service to Christ and others. Paul stated it well in Phil. 3:13-14: "Brethren, I do not count myself to have apprehended; but one thing I do, forgetting those things which are behind and reaching forward to those things which are ahead, I press toward the goal for the prize of

the upward call of God in Christ Jesus." As we try to forget those past experiences that can defeat us, we must remember our text tells us how we can overcome them: "...looking unto Jesus."

Believers should learn and avoid repeating past mistakes and sins. They are not to be defeated by past failures. Many persons are in a confused state because they are bound by little faith and little spiritual service *because of their past* and people or factors that *hurt them* in that past. This writer has found individuals and groups, even in churches, who were angry at fellow believers because of things that occurred in the distant or recent past. Christians are to forgive and seek harmony with others. Christ put this in clear focus when He said in Mt. 6:14-15: "For if you forgive men their trespasses, your heavenly Father will also forgive you. But if you do not forgive men their trespasses, neither will your Father forgive your trespasses."

To grasp fully the rich meaning of Christ's teachings on prayer and forgiveness, it is most important for all of us to know the other precious teachings of Christ in Chapter 6 of Matthew. They are deep truths that bring forth Christ's words on the type of Christian citizens and believers we are to be in His kingdom. God wants Christians to overcome—with the aid of His power—past sins between themselves and others and the lack of meaningful service for Christ's kingdom. God's word tells us that even if our sins are as scarlet, God can wash them away and make them white as snow (Is. 1:18). In the forgiveness of sin, in helping the person who had once been faithful but has since been guilty of great evil thoughts and actions, God's word tells us He will forgive (John 5:24).

3. Faith is the third great force that can lift us out of past and present sins and use us in Christian service once we truly repent and turn from whatever is separating us from fellowship with other believers and our God. Consider the life of the apostle Paul. Early in his life he tried to stamp out those who were believers in Christ. Then he met the Lord in a

vision on the Damascus road; and after that life-changing experience, he spent the rest of his life working for his Lord. He was not only a worker; he was completely dedicated to serving Christ. This was a most difficult task for Paul to pursue; but he had learned that by faith it could be done. His faith and God's power empowered him.

God can help us overcome our environment. By faith He can supply the strength, guidance, the spiritual power, and the leadership we must have for His service. Faith is a great force needed for victory over one's surroundings.

Perhaps our greatest need in this life is a dynamic, strong faith that does not waver. To forget past sins, to ask God to forgive a wasted past and spiritual opportunities neglected or misused, a person needs a strong faith in Christ and His word (John 15:5-10). We must remember that faith is the victory that overcomes the world. Heb. 11:6 says: "But without faith it is impossible to please Him, for he who comes to God must believe that He is, and that He is a rewarder of those who diligently seek Him." Rom. 10:17 tells how to get faith: "So then faith comes by hearing and hearing by the word of God."

Hebrews 11:1 states that "Faith is the substance of things hoped for, the evidence of things not seen." What we can easily see is really only a small part of our world. We cannot see air or electricity, but we can see the results of their energy and work. Faith in Christ and our Father, God, is like that. The Holy Spirit works like that. Faith is having the vision to see what God would have us believe, become, and do. The Holy Spirit supplies the vision and power. It gives sight to our inner spirit; and we see with our brain and imagination what, when, where, and how God can use us and what He would have us do.

In the above we have stressed that believers can overcome the forces of evil that often surround them—those destructive forces that seek to control minds and hearts. The ones discussed are factors that make individuals either Godly, obedient, faithful disciples of Christ or, when not practiced, lacking in knowledge of God's word, unfaithful in responsibility to the living Lord, and poor witnesses for Christ. This then causes them to be drifters in spiritual things, and the peace of God and the joy of the Lord are not a part of their lives.

God has always done His part, and each day He pleads with each of us to do ours. And what is our part? It is to believe, to trust, to venture out in service and devotion—*looking unto Him*. And always this should be done with the prayer: "Teach me to do your will, For you are my God; Your Spirit is good. Lead me in the land of uprightness (Ps. 143:10). This can be done in our lives as we "Look unto Jesus."

CHAPTER 11

CHRISTIAN PROBLEM SOLVING

SCRIPTURAL BACKGROUND: Philippians 4:1-13

TEXT: Phil. 4:6 "Be anxious for nothing, but in everything by prayer and supplication, with thanksgiving, let your requests be made known to God."

Everybody has problems, and Christians are no exception. In fact, sometimes people say their problems are great enough to "worry them to death." Others say theirs are "driving them crazy." Did you notice when you read the text that it deals with one's attitudes, mental set, and spiritual condition? Indeed, in this Scripture passage Paul was dealing with spiritual and mental issues. In Verse 1 he exhorted the Philippians to "stand fast in the Lord," and he spoke to them as "my beloved and longed-for brethren." In Verse 2 he pled for two members of the Philippian church to "be of the same mind in the Lord." In other words, he was asking for unity in the church at Philippi. This exhortation was also made in Phil. 3:16b: "Let us be of the same mind." In Phil. 4:3 he urged the Philippians to *help* the two who were at odds with each other. In Verses 4-9 he wrote about *rejoicing, gentleness,* anxiousness, prayer, thanksgiving, "the peace of God"; things that are true, noble, just, pure, lovely, of good report, virtue, anything praiseworthy; and he concluded with "the God of peace will be with you." These are clearly factors that are concerns of the mind and spiritual condition and welfare of Christians—then and now.

Some biblical scholars have said that these are rules for living; and, indeed, they are. Still, however, they are goals that call for Christians to create—with the help of the Holy Spirit—a living, faithful witness of the Christ who lives within their hearts. But, as many have learned the hard way, often these greatly to be desired mental and spiritual characteristics are not present in our minds, hearts, and lives. In other words, we have difficulty trying to live the elements found in the text even when we seek to rely on Christ's keeping power as stated in the 7th verse of Phil. 4. Also we find it most troublesome to "stand fast in the Lord," as Paul urged the Philippians to do.

Being faithful then—and now—was a great challenge. Misunderstandings then—as now—often confused and divided believers. Paul stated that we are to "rejoice in the Lord" at all times and let our gentleness (kindness) be known to "all men." This is often very hard to do even when we remember that "the Lord is at hand," but he followed it with Phil. 4:6, our text: "Be anxious for nothing, but in everything by prayer and supplication, with thanksgiving, let your requests be made known to God."

Through the ages Christians have *turned to prayer* for comfort, strength, help, and assurance as they sought God's help for the trials, cares, and problems of life. Jesus in His model prayer taught His disciples to pray for "daily bread," forgiveness of sins, forgiveness of others, for help in overcoming and avoiding temptations, deliverance from evil, and recognition that God has the power, glory, and might to rule over His kingdom. True prayer is earnest communion with our heavenly Father. Paul in our text emphasized praying with supplication and thanksgiving. Real prayer to God is making humble and earnest requests to the One—God—who hears and answers prayer; and it is to be done "with thanksgiving." This is taught in many places in the Old and New Testament.

But prayers often seem to go unanswered. Indeed, we sometimes ask, as Job did: "What profit do we have if we pray to Him?" (Job 21:15b). This presents another problem that believers through the ages have encountered: The fact that we do not have the "peace of God which surpasses all understanding" that Paul wrote about in Verse 7 which "will guard your hearts and minds through Christ Jesus." In Ps. 66:18 David gave one major cause of unanswered prayer and also one of the major reasons we have *problems and little or no* "peace of God." He pointed to sin in one's heart. Many references can be found in the Scriptures which make this abundantly clear. David's prayer in Ps. 66:18 is a classic example of this. He said: "If I regard iniquity in my heart, the Lord will not hear." This follows Ps. 66:17 which clearly brings out that David was speaking of worship, praise, and prayer: "I cried to Him with my mouth, and He was extolled with my tongue." Then in Verses 19-20 he continued: "But certainly God has heard me; He has attended to the voice of my prayer." Thus we can think and believe that *earnest prayer* is a major source of power for problem solving. Jesus said: "So I say to you, ask, and it will be given to you; seek, and you will find; knock, and it will be opened to you" (Mt. 7:7).

Praying in keeping with the biblical truths about prayer is a major way to seek a solution to problems. There is another major resource to use in attempting to solve problems. We can *use our minds*, our God given intelligence, our power to think, our power to reason, and to learn from past experiences. A good example of this is in the book of Judges. An Israelite named Joash suddenly found himself in big trouble (Judg. 6:25-32). Joash and his son, Gideon, were farmers. They and others around them had good crops; but before they could harvest them, their enemies, the Midianites and Amalekites, "the people of the East" (Judg. 7:13), would rush in either to destroy or steal them. Gideon received a vision and a message about these people, and the angel of the Lord told him that "the Lord is with you, you mighty man of valor!"(Judg. 6:12). Gideon then spoke to the angel, saying: "O my Lord, if the Lord is with us, why then has all this happened to us?"

Actually Gideon, Joash, and all of Israel had already been told by a special prophet why they were having problems with their enemies and their harvest (Judg. 6:1-12). They had combined the worship of the true and powerful God, Yahweh, with the gods of the Canaanites, Baal false gods, of which there were many. This combination was a direct offense against God's commandments and a very serious affront to God's goodness, mercies, and leadership of Israel in the past. Gideon was told to tear down and burn the false gods and to construct a new altar to Yahweh; but in doing this, he and his father, Joash, got into trouble with their own people. Indeed, Gideon was about to be killed by the people of the city. It was then that Joash used his *mind and moral courage.* He asked the people: "Would you plead for Baal? Would you save him? Let the one who would plead for him be put to death by morning! If he is a god, let him plead for himself" (Judg. 6:31). Joash was appealing to their reasoning power.

This speech by Joash struck a nerve with the people. They remembered the first commandment Moses had received from God and given to them. They were to have no other gods before their true God, Yahweh. In their minds they were convicted of their lack of faith in Yahweh and their belief that the gods of Baal were needed.

The point to be made here is that often we create big problems for ourselves—physical, financial, mental, and spiritual—by our lack of faith and by bringing into our lives those forces that we know in our hearts and minds are destructive. What are some of these? Too much food of the wrong kind and too little of the right kind create health problems. No, I am not saying we create all of our physical problems; but we surely cause some of them. The abuse of drugs can produce much heartache for ourselves, friends, loved ones, and society in general. The abuse of alcohol is another classic example. When Christians and others fill their minds with lustful thinking, greed, selfishness, and think only of themselves at the expense of others, they create problems for themselves and others. This writer also believes that we create a spiritual wasteland for ourselves when we neglect the reading and studying of God's word, prayer, and helping—doing what we can for others. Yes, we need to pray about problems and to seek God's help in all of the above; but God appeals to our minds, past experiences, and our abilities to reason. Again, what we are saying is that God is an ever present help; but He expects His people to know and follow His laws and words, not to *earn salvation*, but to abide in Him, His word, and what His word says about the way to conduct themselves in this life. God's word and the use of one's mind for godly living can also keep Christians away from many problems.

God's presence and the Holy Spirit can help in solving problems. God's power is supreme; but unbelief and evil in our hearts and lives can result in spiritual bankruptcy, confusion, and serious consequences in the form of problems. On the other hand, God's presence in our lives can sharpen our intellectual ability, not only to help us solve problems, but also to avoid them.

David was a gifted and talented person; but, when led by his own lust and power as king, he set aside what he knew was the right way to live and ended up committing the very serious crimes of adultery and murder. He also lost his close fellowship with God. He did not repent of these sins until God's prophet, Nathan, stood before him and confronted him with the awfulness of what he had done. Then he acknowledged his transgressions and repented—changed his mind with sorrow in his heart—for what he had done. Ps. 51:1-2 tells of this: "Have mercy upon me, O God, according to Your lovingkindness, according to the multitude of Your tender mercies, Blot out my transgressions. Wash me thoroughly from my iniquity, and cleanse me from my sin." In his prayer for forgiveness he said: "My sin is always before me (in his mind and heart). Against You, You only have I sinned, and done this evil in Your sight" (Ps. 51:3-4). Verses 10-11 should also be studied in connection with his mental struggle, repentance, and his desire for God to create in him "a clean heart," and to "renew a steadfast spirit within me." In Verse 11 he further prayed that God would not "cast me away from Your presence, and" take His Holy Spirit from him. Ps. 51:13-17 speaks to us also about one's mental and spiritual service to God then and now. These verses remind us that repentance comes first—even before great sacrifices. Then, and only then, can we praise, worship, pray, and serve God. "The sacrifices of God are a broken spirit, a broken and a contrite heart—These, O God, You will not despise" (Ps. 51:17).

Now, some who read this may be asking why there is all this concern about mental and spiritual problem solving. To this writer it is the central issue. We are controlled by our minds and our attitudes. Even repentance—true repentance—involves them. As many Scriptures teach, our prayers, worship, praise, and service are controlled by our minds and attitudes—toward God. Truly, as we think in our minds and hearts, that is what we are. In this connection think of Zech. 4:6: "'Not by might nor by power, but by My spirit' says the Lord of Hosts." This is the attitude and mental set that we must maintain in worship, praise, service, and Christian problem solving.

Think again of the people of Israel in Gideon's day. They—in their minds and hearts—had forgotten what God, Yahweh, had done for them in the past and present. God had not forgotten them. He was still helping them grow crops and cattle, but they had adopted Baal and the worship of false gods. It seems they had done this without giving it much thought. They just tacked on to their worship of God the worship of Baal; so God let their enemies take and destroy their harvest. He used Joash and Gideon to help them remember—in their hearts and minds—the true God. When they changed their minds about Baal worship and false gods, God used Gideon and his army to drive out the enemies of Israel. We should never think, however, that we are so gifted and intelligent that we, using our own minds, can always solve our own problems. We cannot. Every day and every hour we need God's power, presence, and guidance. At all times we should remember that we need Him for spiritual and mental problems—for truly, without Him we can do nothing.

In the paragraph above we stated that always we need God's power, presence, and guidance. The words of Christ as given in John 8:12 can aid us as we seek help in problem solving and guidance: "Then Jesus spoke to them again saying, 'I am the light of the world. He who follows Me shall not walk in darkness, but have the light of life'." Those who follow and look to Jesus and His teachings as their guide and strength truly have the light of life. They also cherish Phil. 4:5b: "The Lord is at hand." In the Old Testament God provided light, guidance, and assurance of His presence with a pillar of fire for the children of Israel in their wilderness wanderings. Today Jesus assures us that He will be a source of light and power in our lives for problem solving, power, and guidance. "He who follows Me shall not walk in darkness" (John 3:12b).

Consider also the following: In Ps. 27:1 David said: "The Lord is my light and my salvation; whom shall I fear? The Lord is the strength of my life; of whom shall I be afraid?" The prophet, Micah, said: "When I sit in darkness, the Lord will be a light to me" (Mic. 7:8). Isaiah told the people of his day: "The Lord will be to you an everlasting light, and your God your glory" (Is. 60:19b). In our troubles, difficulties, problem solving, and need for guidance and strength, remember He is the light of the world and, as the hymn writer, Will L. Thompson wrote: "He is my strength from day to day, without Him I would fall." The apostle Peter speaks to us about problem solving: "Casting all your care upon Him, for He cares for you (1 Pet. 5:7).

SUMMARY AND CONCLUSION

Some of the major ways *Christians* can solve problems are as follows:

- "In everything by prayer…let your requests be known to God" (Phil. 4:6).
- Use your own God-given minds under the leadership of the Holy Spirit to think, reason, evaluate, and draw on your experience.
- Use God's presence and power (Phil. 6:13). He has promised always to be with the believer—"in every condition."
- Seek God's help and the use of His word in solving problems in *every aspect* of your life. Live what God's word says about loving, forgiving, serving, and relating to others. Take Phil. 4:6 seriously; it is part of God's word, the Bible. Avoid hate and prejudice—let Christ be your example in dealing with others.

ADDENDUM

The Essence of Faith

"What we can easily see is only a small percentage of what is possible. Faith is having the vision to see what is just below the surface; to picture that which is essential but invisible to the eye."

The apostle Paul wrote about similar ideas in 1 Cor. 2:9-10. This is the way he stated it: "'...Eye has not seen, nor ear heard, Nor have entered into the heart of man The things which God has prepared for those who love Him.' But God has revealed them to us through His Spirit. For the Spirit searches all things, yes, the deep things of God."

Let us strive for a vision of what God wants us to be and do with our lives. We can best do this by obedience, study of His word, and constant prayer. "Teach me to do Your will, For You are my God; Your Spirit is good. Lead me in the land of uprightness" (Ps. 143:10).

CHAPTER 12

CHRISTIAN PROBLEM SOLVING IN HUMAN RELATIONS

SCRIPTURAL BACKGROUND: Phil. 3:7-14 and Phil. 4:4-9

TEXT: Phil. 4:6 "Be anxious for nothing, but in everything by prayer and supplication, with thanksgiving, let your requests be made known to God."

In the previous message an endeavor was made to consider prayerfully some of the ways a Christian believer could attempt to solve problems. In this message the writer wants to continue sharing ways that he has found effective in solving some of the most trying of personal problems; yet, he wants it understood that it is not possible to improve on what God has already said in His Holy word about solving problems, cares, and difficulties.

1 Peter 5:7 speaks to this topic: "casting all your care upon Him, for he cares for you." John 14:6a gives help in the face of problems, misunderstandings, and difficulties: "...I am the way, the truth, and the life." John 14:16 says: "And I will pray the Father, and He will give you another Helper, that He may abide with you forever." The Holy Spirit—sent by God—is ever present for the trusting believer. He is our helper, guide, provider, and strength. He can work far beyond any earthly power

to comfort, sustain, and help in times of sorrow, pain, confusion, oppression, grief, and trouble. These are human relations challenges.

In the previous message this writer stated several specific ways for Christians to approach solving problems:

    Be in constant and sincere prayer (Phil. 4:6).

    Use your own God-given mind with the aid of the Holy Spirit to think, reason, evaluate, and learn from experience.

    Depend on and use God's presence and power (Phil. 6:13).

    Try to live what the Scriptures have to say about loving, serving, and relating to others.

Having said this, let us look at Christian problem solving in some of the most difficult areas of life—the ones that pertain to human relations. These problems can be in the home, community, workplace, politics, and, yes, even churches. Many of these are filled with strife, hatred, lack of concern for others, and selfishness.

In Phil. 4:6a Paul made a strong statement, and indeed, he set a very high goal for any believer in any age. He said: "Be anxious for nothing." Now this is a most difficult request for most of us, and it surely gives us reason for thought. The word, *anxious*, means to be full of anxiety, or to worry due to apprehension; or the fear and anticipation of misfortune, danger, or the future. In today's world with the uncertainties and problems that face Christians and non-Christians, can we really take these words seriously? One of the major themes of the four gospels is *fear not*. In that spirit let us consider *some* of the ways Christians can face the future and the problems to be solved. And, let us again use as the central theme—our text—Phil. 4:6. Think of it prayerfully. Keep it uppermost in your mind as you read this message. "Be anxious for nothing, but in everything by prayer and supplication, with thanksgiving, let your requests be made known to God."

Human relations problems may be caused by many reasons. In some cases they become so great that the persons involved leave. For example, half of the marriages in the United States end in divorce. Sometimes communities are so stressed by crime, hate, prejudice, and poverty that members of such communities cannot solve them. There are problems in the workplace caused by excessive demands by employers, managers, and bosses; sexual harassment; and employees who will not do their share of the work. Often forces in politics and government are oppressive and dishonest. These hurt people and rob them of their livelihood. Yes, even in places of worship, problems that divide, hurt, and offend can arise.

How does the Christian go about solving such challenges? To this writer the first thing is to realize that alone we are not able to solve many of them. There are Christian parents who have failed in their serious and prolonged efforts to help their rebellious children. Believers often try to provide for the needy and handicapped, but still fail in their efforts. Often they find themselves in private companies and government organizations that have leaders, managers, and executives who are dishonest, unthoughtful, oppressive, and unconcerned for others. How do Christians respond to such problems? Again—as stated above—by prayer and by using their minds, they can meet challenges.

There are other ways, and some of them are as follows:

> Turn to the Scriptures. Know and try—with the help of God's power and presence—to live them. James 1:22a says: "But be doers of the word, and not hearers only."
>
> Avoid hate and prejudice. This might best be done by remembering that we are to love others as we love ourselves. This is sometimes difficult to do. It can be helpful, however, to think of 1 John 4:19-20: "We love Him because He first loved us." In the next verse is found these words: "If someone says, 'I love God,' and hates his brother, he is a liar; for he who does not love his brother whom he has seen,

how can he love God whom he has not seen?" Eph. 5:1-2 is helpful on this topic: "Therefore be *imitators* of God as dear children, and walk in love, as Christ also has loved us and given Himself for us…" Avoiding hate and prejudice is not an easy thing to do because so much of this is deeply ingrained in our minds and attitudes; and in so many ways we have learned prejudice from an early age in life.

In our attempts to fight and avoid these negative forces we can gain support that pertains to communities, units of government, and even religious bodies from Jer. 29:7: "…Seek the peace of the city *where I have caused you to be carried away captive, and pray to the Lord for it*; for in its peace you will have peace." To this writer these words just quoted mean that if we are seeking to be faithful followers of Christ, God has had a hand in placing us wherever we are living; and He can use us in our present and future dwelling place. It also means that we are to try to improve our lives, the lives of family and loved ones, the community in which we live; and we are to be involved in seeking to better our environment and society. We are to seek and pray for God's help and leadership in all our efforts.

Avoid procrastination. Many of us have a natural or habitual tendency to procrastinate—to delay, to put things off for another day or time. We often look for "a more convenient season" as Felix, the Roman ruler of Paul's day did (Acts 24:25). This practice, in many cases, results in the work for Christ and our service to others not getting done. The procrastination—the delaying of what should be done—in our home life, workplace, civic duties, and Christian service often causes us to fall far short of what we could be doing for Christ, others, and the work of His kingdom. What can we do about the habit and tendency to delay or never do the things our minds and hearts tell us we should be doing in human relations?

One suggestion is to evaluate our use of time. Perhaps we are not taking time for prayer, Bible reading, or service to God and others. Perhaps we need to read and take to heart the words of the great hymn, "Take Time to Be Holy." Another hymn worth our praying and thinking about is "Open My Eyes That I May See," written many years ago by Clara N. Scott. Remember Jesus once said to those who were His disciples and to seventy others also: "The harvest truly is great, but the laborers are few; therefore pray the Lord of the harvest to send out *laborers into His harvest*" (Luke 10:2).

The need for those who would work today for Christ is great, as it was in biblical times. Many times we procrastinate because we are discouraged or our love and fellowship has grown cold, or we have been too occupied with other things at home or outside the home. Perhaps we need to remember that we are to be light and salt in our world.

Sometimes we procrastinate because we feel that there is little we can do. We underestimate our abilities and opportunities and become discouraged. Jeremiah was like this once, and God said to him: "Call to me, and I will answer you, and show you great and *mighty* things, which you do not know" (Jer. 33:3). When we are discouraged, defeated, and unable to solve the problems which confront us; we need to remember God is always ready to help if we call to Him. In this connection, let us not forget that God cannot use us to solve problems of our own and of others "if our lives are not free from known sins; We will barriers be and a hindrance to those we are trying to win" and help, as stated in the great hymn, "Make Me a Channel of Blessings."

Our text tells us to "be anxious for nothing, but in everything by prayer and supplication, with thanksgiving, let your requests be known to God." Christians are to pray about religious, social, business, family, mental, physical, and personal problems. They should never forget Phil. 4:13: "I can do all things through Christ who strengthens me." These words do not mean that God is going to make us rich if we think we should be, or that He is going to strengthen us to become great and famous in whatever worldly area we dream up. The Bible is a spiritual book. It is concerned with man's need for God's salvation through Jesus Christ, his need to know God and His fellowship through the Holy Spirit, and his need for spiritual knowledge and faith built on God's truth and terms.

Another major way that Christians can solve difficulties is by way of *problem identification*. Some believers are *poor* and their families are in need because they *wasted the money* God helped them earn. Many indeed are impoverished, but often their real *problem* is one of mismanaging what God has given them. Once a man, a member of my church, told me how wonderful he now thought our church was; how he was saving *money*, yet providing more *money* for the church and his loved ones than ever before. I, of course, had to ask him: "How are you doing all of this?" He quickly replied: "I quit my constant abuse of alcohol and tobacco." He identified his problem; then he could, as he said, ask for God's forgiveness, for His help in the areas just mentioned, for help in a closer walk with Him, and His guidance in finding ways to serve his Savior and Lord. He had identified his problem and, as the young prodigal son did, he came to himself, used his God-given power to reason, think, remember, and return to his Father, God.

In problem identification we should prayerfully ask God to guide us in our thinking and actions. Often Christians try to *explain away* problems. They, as mental health workers and psychologists say, try to rationalize why they are having difficulties. Some people really are poor; but as we saw above, many try to excuse or blame their problems on causes other than the real one. When David sinned and was finally confronted by Nathan, he immediately stated that he was guilty of murder and adultery. He said to God: "Against You, You only, have I sinned, and done this evil in Your sight" (Ps. 51:4a). Christians today have many *excuses* or *rationalizations* they use to try to explain away the real causes for lack of *giving* and serving, and the failure of faithfulness to God, church, family, and others. They like to blame the environment, poor education, too little or too much money, a materialistic society, too little ability, not enough time, and on and on we could go; yet the real reason may be violation of the first two commandments and the refusal to make Christ *Savior and Lord* of their lives.

The final suggestion for Christian problem solving is *steadfast Christian living*. In 1 Cor. 15:58 we find Paul's words of advice: "...be steadfast, immovable, always abounding in the work of the Lord, knowing that your labor is not in vain in the Lord." Just before he wrote that verse, he said in Verse 57: "But thanks be to God, who gives us the victory through our Lord Jesus Christ." Now in both verses he was speaking of first, victory over death (Verse 57), then faithfulness and steadfastness in one's Christian walk and service (Verse 58). The life of a Christian cannot be a thing of joy, peace, or fruitfulness if the person living it is wishy-washy, an on and off person, seemingly a sincere believer at one time but speaking and living in non-Christian ways at other times.

We Christians know we are saved by God's grace and mercy—but we are also to live for Him who died for us. We are to love the Lord our God and love others as we love ourselves. This is a tremendous challenge. We must be steadfast for Christ, His work, and others. You ask: "But what does that have to do with Christian problem solving?" My answer is *"everything."* We pray for strength, peace, help in trouble, human relations problems, and God's guidance for our lives. These things can be possible when we abide in Him; but His grace, peace, joy, and presence cannot be ours *if we are unstable in the faith* and live only for worldly pleasures, money, power, and other things that would set forth our profession of faith as something that is to be taken lightly. Steadfast Christian living is necessary in good Christian human relations.

Summary and Conclusions

Ask God for help in solving problems in human relations:
- a. Call upon Him; He has promised to hear and answer.
- b. Strive to avoid judging others.
- c. Pray for others; forgive others; let Christ be your example.

> d. Avoid the tendency to delay, to put off, to procrastinate in doing for others what you know you should do.

Evaluate your attitudes, Christian witness, and service to Christ and others.

Evaluate how you are using the time and opportunities God has given you.

Try to do what Phil. 4:6 says: "Be anxious for nothing, but in everything by prayer and supplication, with thanksgiving, let your requests be known to God."

Try to think through and identify your human relations problems and their causes, not just their results. Some examples are as follows:

> a. Money mismanagement—results can be debts and poverty.
>
> b. Alcohol and drug abuse—results can be addiction, slavery to them, broken homes, ruined lives, and wasted resources.
>
> c. Forgetting one's need for God, worship, prayer, thanksgiving, and knowledge of God's word—results can be confusion; a sense of feeling powerless; loneliness; and a lack of Christian fellowship, God's peace, and joy in one's salvation.

Try—with the Lord's help and the guidance of the Holy Spirit—to live a steadfast Christian life. 1 Cor. 15:58 states: "...be steadfast, immovable, always abounding in the work of the Lord, knowing that your labor is not in vain in the Lord." How can we be steadfast in a compromising and materialistic world? In our own strength we cannot; but Ps. 121:2 tells us: "...my help comes from the Lord." In Eph.

6:10-18 Paul, in very honest and bold words, stated how to be steadfast and faithful:
- a. "Be strong in the Lord and in the power of His might: (Verse 10).
- b. "Put on the whole armor of God, that you may be able to stand..." (Verse 11).

Walking by faith, try to seek God's will and guidance in solving problems in human relations.

John 14:16: "And I will pray the Father, and He will give you another Helper (the Holy Spirit), that He may abide with you forever."

John 15:12: "This is My commandment, that you love one another as I have loved you."

If we truly love God and one another, this type of love, with prayer and knowledge of God's word, will go a long way in solving challenging Christian problems in human relations.

CHAPTER 13

JESUS AS THE WAY, THE TRUTH, AND THE LIFE

SCRIPTURAL BACKGROUND: John 14:1-21

TEXT: John 14:6 "...I am the way, the truth, and the life."

The book of John was written to inspire and help believers of his day have a deeper and greater faith in the Lord and Savior, Jesus Christ. Many biblical scholars consider John 20:30-31 to be the key verses of this New Testament account of the gospel. It reads: "And truly Jesus did many other signs in the presence of His disciples, which are not written in this book; but these are written that you may believe that Jesus is the Christ, the Son of God, and that believing you may have life in His name." This writer feels that it is important to remember that John was a beloved apostle of Jesus. John's gospel is thought by many students of the New Testament to be the deepest, most thought-provoking, and most spiritual book in the Bible. John, inspired and enlightened by the Spirit of God, gave an excellent, complete, and meaningful revelation of Jesus and of God.[7]

There are many truths in this account of the gospel, but in this message we want to concentrate on the text, John 14:6, in which Jesus said: "...I am the way, the truth, and the life." There is a danger in lifting one verse of Scripture for analysis, but this danger can be avoided if the setting and background of the verse is understood. For that reason this writer sincerely recommends that readers study all of John, Chapter 14, as well as Chapters 12 through 17. This, when done prayerfully, will be time well spent.

When Jesus said: "I am the way, the truth, and the life," it was a critical time in His ministry; and His disciples were very troubled. They evidently were still expecting Jesus to drive out the Roman invaders of Israel, their homeland, and set up some sort of powerful political kingdom. Judas—who carried and stole from the money bag—was especially concerned with this, according to many biblical authorities. They have said that this belief was one of the primary reasons he betrayed Jesus. They believe that Judas was trying to force Him to confront the Jewish religious leaders of the day because he believed that Jesus, in such a confrontation, would work some miracle, put down the scribes and Pharisees, and force out the Roman invaders. This, however, was not the way the Son of God was to establish His kingdom. His kingdom was to be and is a spiritual one.

What did Jesus mean when He said: "I am the way"? One meaning is clearly stated in Verse 6, which contains our text. In it He stated: "No one comes to the Father except through me." In other words, He is the way of salvation and eternal life. Jesus told Nicodemus that "God so loved…that He gave His only begotten Son, that whoever believes in Him should not perish but have everlasting life" (John 3:16). Acts 4:12 points out that "there is no other name under heaven given among men by which we must be saved." Mt. 7:14 tells us that "narrow is the gate and difficult is the way which leads to life"; and this statement is explained by what Jesus taught in the previous verse: "Enter by the narrow gate; for wide is the gate and broad is the way that leads to destruction." This is further clarified in Verses 24-27 in which He gave the parable of the wise and the foolish builders. Jesus is the Christian's "Rock of ages" and blessed assurance for eternity. The hymn writer, George Keith, wrote about this:

> "How firm a foundation, ye saints of the Lord,
> Is laid for your faith in His excellent word!
> What more can He say than to you He hath said,
> To you, who for refuge to Jesus have fled."[8]

In Mt. 7:15-23 Jesus shed light on why He referred to *His way* as a difficult and narrow way. Paul, In Rom. 3:12 quoted from Ps. 14:3 when he stated: "They have all turned aside...there is none who does good, no, not one." But in Verse 22 of the same chapter he set forth the *way out of* sin and unprofitableness: "Even the righteousness of God, through faith in Jesus Christ, to all and on all who believe." In Acts 16:17 when Paul, Silas, and Timothy were preaching at Philippi, a slave girl kept following them around the city; and she cried out, much to the distress of her owners: "These men are the servants of the Most High God, who proclaim to us *the way* of salvation." That way was the Jesus *way*.

Acts 18:24-26 testifies to Jesus as the way of salvation. These verses tell of "a certain Jew named Apollos, born at Alexandria...fervent in spirit...though he knew only the baptism of John.... When Aquila and Priscilla heard him, they took him aside and explained to him the *way* of God more accurately." That *way* was what Apollos preached after he was told of Jesus' death and resurrection, and Acts 18:28 says: "He vigorously refuted the Jews publicly, sharing from the Scriptures that Jesus is the Christ."

Paul wrote of Jesus in Heb. 10:20 as "a new and living way which He consecrated for us, through the veil, that is, His flesh." In Verse 23 of that chapter he said: "Let us hold fast the confession of our hope without wavering, for He who promised is faithful." Heb. 12:2 refers to Christ as "the author and finisher of our faith, who for the joy that was set before

Him endured the cross, despising the shame, and has sat down at the right hand of the throne of God." Jessie Brown Pounds wrote of Jesus, His cross, and the way in her great hymn, "The Way of the Cross Leads Home." Here are some of the words of that hymn:

"I must needs go home by the way of the cross, There's no other way but this;
I shall ne'er get sight of the Gates of Light, If the way of the cross I miss.
The way of the cross leads home; It is sweet to know, as I onward go,
The way of the cross leads home."[9]

In 2 Pet. 2:17 is found an excellent description of the individual who does not believe in Jesus as the way: "These are wells without water, clouds carried by a tempest, for whom is reserved the blackness of darkness forever." In other words—speaking in a spiritual sense—they are of little value compared to believers who have eternal life now and through eternity.

In 1 Pet. 1:3 there is a most important message in connection with Christ as the way to eternal life. It reads this way: "Blessed be the God and Father of our Lord Jesus Christ, who according to His abundant mercy has begotten us again to a living hope through the resurrection of Jesus Christ from the dead." The Christian's "living hope" is centered on Jesus Christ—His death on the cross and His resurrection from the grave. We believe Him and what He said as recorded in John 14:19b: "Because I live, you will live also." As born again believers we are loved by God, forgiven of our sins, and heirs to eternal life through faith in Christ.

In our "modern" world we are confronted with all kinds of distractions and constantly exposed to all sorts of ambiguities, temptations, and frustrations; however, we are always aware of His nearness and presence. We also remember Paul's comforting words in Rom. 8:28: "And

Does God Care about You and Me?

we know that all things work together for good to those who love God, to those who are the called according to His purpose." We further find assurance, comfort, and strength in Rom. 8:31b: "If God is for us, who can be against us?" And Rom. 8:34b tells that Christ is now "at the right hand of God, who also makes intercession for us."

Paul follows these tremendous truths by proclaiming in Verses 37-39b: "Yet in all these things we are more than conquerors through Him who loved us. For I am persuaded that neither death nor life, nor angels nor principalities nor powers, nor things present nor things to come, nor height nor depth, nor any other created things, shall be able to separate us from the love of God which is in Christ Jesus our Lord."

Christ is the *way* to eternal life. In our dangerous world of the 21st century with its wars, diseases, and hideous crimes, we are still assured of His presence and of eternal life. We are still children of the living God who will always be in charge of His world. Even in the presence of death and destruction we can know that He loves, cares, and will provide for us. Thus with the assurance of His words—"I will never forsake you"—we can face today and the future knowing that Jesus truly is our way and the life. With this realization of God's word we know that God is always present; thus our faith in Him is strengthened and our hope is securely anchored in Christ.

Our text, John 14:6, has another major element that Christ proclaimed to the disciples and the world. He said: "…I am the…truth." In the very first chapter of his gospel John had said: "And the Word became flesh and dwelt among us, and we beheld His glory, the glory as of the only begotten of the Father, full of grace and truth" (John 1:14). And in John 8:31b and 32 Jesus had already stated: "If you abide in My word, you are My disciples indeed. And you shall know the *truth*, and the truth shall make you free." Clearly, Jesus is referring to Himself and His sacrifice for the sins of the world. In Verse 36 of the same chapter He continues to refer to Himself as the One—the truth—who sets believers free: "Therefore if the Son makes you free, you shall be free indeed."

It is a very rewarding and worshipful experience to think of Christ, the truth, who sets the believer free. Because of God's love for us and because of Christ Jesus—God's sacrifice for our sins—we can be free from the following and much, much more:

> Free from sin that can separate one from God—now and through eternity—John 3:16-17.
>
> Free from the fear and dread of death.
>
> Free from the chains and guilt of past sins—whatever they are. As Charles Wesley wrote:
>
> "He breaks the power of canceled sin, Blessed be the name of the Lord!
>
> His blood can make the foulest clean, Blessed be the name of the Lord!"[10]
>
> Free from self condemnation and burdens of guilt.
>
> Free from inferior complexes and feelings of inadequacy.
>
> Free from the uncertainty of the future.
>
> Free from believing that the world, its false value system of greed, distrust, little gods, and broken promises are to be our goals.
>
> Free from the force of enslaving habits that drain away our strength, time, and spiritual power, and handicap our Christian witness and service.
>
> Free from believing that these false forces should control our lives.

Christ—as the truth—brings the believer into the real circle of reality:

The fact of a holy, just, and merciful God.

The fact of God as the creator and sustainer of the universe and life on this earth.

The fact of sin on the part of man and his need for God's mercy and forgiveness.

Jesus Christ and His word are truth as stated in our text: "...I am the way, the truth, and the life." His person and presence are the bases of the Christian's faith, hope, love, and courage. He is our redeemer, Savior, and friend. Christ, the truth, is constant and consistent in every way and always ready to fulfill His work and promises in the lives of believers. He is the revelation of God and as such, that revelation is always available to those who seek to live and serve in His love and will.

In the above discussion we have considered Christ as the *way* to God and the *truth* of God revealed in Him—His sinless life, His powerful resurrection, His constant presence, and His unchanging love. Let us now consider the third main element in our text. Jesus said: "...I am... the life" (John 14:6). What did Jesus mean when He stated that He is "the life"? Surely, He must have meant that He is the sinless revelation of the perfect life and the way believers are to live their lives. After His resurrection Jesus told His followers: "If anyone loves Me, he will keep My word; and My Father will love him, and We will come to him and make Our home with him" (John 14:23b). He also *promised* the following to those who believe in Him and *abide* in Him:

Peace and freedom from fear: John 14:27 and 16:33.

Power through the Holy Spirit: John 14:26.

Instruction and help through the Holy Spirit: John 14:26 and 16:13.

Power for service: John 14:12.

Answered prayer when asked in His name: John 14:13-14.

> Constant presence of the Holy Spirit: John 14:16-17.
> Eternal life: John 14:1-3, 6.
> Effective Christian service in this life: John 15:5.
> His joy in this present life: John 15:11 and 16:22.
> His friendship: John 15:14-15.
> God's love: John 16:27.
> Unity and oneness with God and other believers: John 17:20-26.

Perhaps the great hymn composer, Philip P. Bliss, had some of these promises in his heart and mind when he wrote the hymn, "Wonderful Words of Life":

"Sing them over again to me, Wonderful words of life;
Let me more of their beauty see, Wonderful words of life;
Words of life and beauty, Teach me faith and duty;
Beautiful words, beautiful words, Wonderful words of life."[11]

Truly, Christ is the life we should strive to live. Not that we can be perfect or sinless, but we should attempt to live our lives in submission and service as He did. He lived His life to redeem us from sin and to glorify His Father in heaven. He came that we might have life and "have it more abundantly" (John 10:10b). Jesus, the Christ, offers us the Holy Spirit who can give us the strength to live for Him who died for all who will believe. It is Christ, and Christ alone, who through His word and sinless life can show us the way to face trials, temptations, and troubles. Faith and hope in our Savior gives us the abundant life in this world and eternal life in the next.

In this life we will have trials, temptations, and troubles; and when these come, we are to remember John 14:1-2: "Let not your heart be troubled; you believe in God, believe also in Me. In My Father's house are many mansions; if it were not so, I would have told you. I go to prepare a place for you." That is our comfort, hope, and assurance. Jesus promised He would never leave us alone. There is more, however. He also promised us the strength to sustain us day by day. Our text, John 14:6, tells in Jesus' own words: "...I am the way, the truth, and the life."

CHAPTER 14

FOUR FRUITS OF THE SPIRIT IN A CHRISTIAN'S LIFE

SCRIPTURAL BACKGROUND: Gal. 5:22-26 and 6:1-10

TEXT: Gal. 5:22-23 "But the fruit of the Spirit is love, joy, peace, longsuffering, kindness, goodness, faithfulness, gentleness, self-control."

Paul's letter to the churches in Galatia has been called by some Bible scholars the Magna Charta of the Christian Church. The dominant topic in this New Testament book is Christian liberty in Christ as opposed to the Old Testament ceremonial law that the so-called Judaizers of that day insisted was necessary for salvation along with faith in Christ as Savior and Lord. Some of the major themes Paul—led by the Holy Spirit—set forth are the following:

Justification is by faith in Jesus Christ alone (3:24).

Christian believers are free from the observance of the ceremonial law (2:1-5).

The purpose of the old ceremonial law, given in the Old Testament, was to be as a tutor: "...the law was our tutor to bring us to Christ, that we might be justified by faith" (3:24-26).

> The works of the flesh war against the spiritual life, and they can prevent a person from inheriting the kingdom of God (5:19-21).
> There are fruits or results which should be apparent in a steadfast Christian life (6:22-26).
> "If we live in the Spirit, let us also walk in the Spirit" (5:25).

These fruits of the Spirit are what this writer would have you think about at this time. Yes, he is very much aware of the fact that many sermons have been preached about each one of the fruits of the Spirit. In this message, however, let your focus be on four of these results of a spiritual life. This should be done with mental sharpness because the topics are crucial for Christian living, God-given peace of mind, and effective Christian service.

Consider what Paul conveyed about the very first of these fruits—the fruit or result of *love*. In 1 Corinthians, Chapter 13, he said that having and using all types of gifts are nothing without love. In fact, he declared that even if he could speak with the tongues of angels and men, it would be just noise without love—Christian love. The gift of prophecy and of understanding all mysteries and all knowledge; and even if he had all faith to remove mountains (problems), it would still amount to nothing without love. In Verse 3 he stated that if one gives all of his earthly goods to the poor and even one's own body to be burned, it is of no profit without love. Then Paul listed some of the things that a Godly Christian love can and does do:

"Love suffers long and is kind;
Love does not envy;
Love does not parade itself; is not puffed up;
Love does not behave rudely; does not seek its own;
Love is not provoked, thinks no evil;
Love does not rejoice in iniquity, but rejoices in the truth;

Love bears all things, believes all things, endures all things. Love never fails. Love is greater than faith and hope."

It is this writer's prayer that you remember John 3:16: "For God so loved…that He gave His only Begotten Son." Remember "we love Him, because He first loved us" (1 John 4:19). Remember the love of God is more than we can express with tongue or pen. "If I had the gift of being able to speak in other languages without learning them, and could speak in every language there is in all of heaven and earth, but did not love others, I would only be making noise" (1 Cor. 13:1, TLB). Consider also Christ's words about the first and second commandments as found in Mt. 22:37-39: "Jesus said to him: 'You shall love the Lord your God with all your heart, with all your soul, and with all your mind. This is the first and great commandment. And the second is like it: You shall love your neighbor as yourself'." All the efforts of many writers who have written about Godly love fall far short of the words of Jesus and the statement of Paul—led by the Holy Spirit—about love.

In Prov. 10:12 is found: "Hatred stirs up strife, but love covers all sins." In Ps. 91:14-15 can be read what God has to say about believers who trust in Him: "Because he has set his love upon me, therefore I will deliver him; I will set him on high, because he has known My name. He shall call upon Me, and I will answer him."

In the New Testament we find Scriptures that speak of the importance of love. Some of the outstanding ones are as follows:

> John 13:34-35: "A new commandment I give to you, that you love one another; as I have loved you, that you also love one another. By this all will know that you are My disciples, if you have love for one another." These words were spoken by Jesus at the Last Supper. They do not demand commentary; they are crystal clear and speak for themselves.
>
> John 15:9-10, 12, 14: "As the Father loved Me, I also have loved

you; abide in My love. If you keep My commandments, you will abide in My love, just as I have kept My Father's commandments and abide in His love.... This is My commandment, that you love one another as I have loved you.... You are My friends if you do whatever I command you." These are simple words, but they were used by the Savior to make powerful statements of truth.

In Rom. 12:9 and 10 the militant, missionary, apostle Paul urged: "Let love be without hypocrisy. Abhor what is evil. Cling to what is good. Be kindly affectionate to one another with brotherly love, in honor giving preference to one another; not lagging in diligence, fervent in spirit, serving the Lord."

Rom. 13:10 elaborates on the above: "Love does no harm to a neighbor; therefore love is the fulfillment of the law."

In 2 Cor. 5:14-15 Paul stated: "For the love of Christ compels us,...that those who live should live no longer for themselves, but for Him who died for them and rose again."

2 Cor. 13:11: "Become complete. Be of good comfort, be of one mind, live in peace; and the God of *love* and peace will be with you." What a great promise and, indeed, what a worthy goal—to have the God of love and peace to be with us!

In Gal. 2:20 Paul said: "I have been crucified with Christ;... but Christ lives in me; and the life which I now live...I live by faith in the Son of God, who loved me and gave Himself for me."

What summation was Paul making? It was that because Christ loved him and died for him; he would live his life on this earth for Jesus, the Christ, the Son of the Living God. Can we as Christians of today afford to do anything less? In the words of a precious old hymn: "What more can He say than to you He has said?" When God's love is allowed to fill our hearts, we will then be ready to serve God and our fellowman. Love of God causes us to seek His way, not our own. Love can make us kind and unselfish, patient and forbearing, free of hate and anger, concerned for social justice, never seeking just our own self-interest.

Joy is the next fruit of the Spirit that Paul set forth. In the English dictionary joy is defined as an emotion of great delight or happiness caused by something good or satisfying. How appropriate that is for the Christian believers. Christians who are concerned with and are living in the Spirit do so because they have great reason for joy—they are children of God and joint heirs with Christ. As stated in 1 John 3:1: "Behold what manner of love the Father has bestowed upon us that we should be called children of God!" Our God is the almighty Father, the omnipresent, omnipotent, all knowing, all loving, all caring God. This is the major reason we have joy.

This joy is not just a moment of happiness because of some good fortune that may have happened to us. It is not an outburst of emotions over some small gain or favor we may have received. Instead, this fruit of the Spirit, *joy*, is the realization that not only have we been saved by God's mercy and grace, but that we have been made children of the Almighty, heirs to eternal life, and citizens in the kingdom of God. Thus we have joy, which is none other than the outward expression of God's grace that we now know we have in our own hearts and lives.

The English dictionary definition of joy has been considered. It is worthwhile to examine the definition as given in the Greek lexicon. The Greek word for joy is *chara*, and *charis* is Greek for grace—God's grace, and guess what! They both come from the same root. What does this mean? What does it say to us? It says to me that as a result of being loved by God, and as a result of His Son, Jesus the Christ, I have reason to rejoice, or as Paul put it in Phil. 4:4: "Rejoice in the Lord always; again

I will say rejoice." Our joy—*spiritual and mental happiness*—comes from knowing that we are not only loved by God; but that we are His children and Jesus Christ, God's Son, will never leave or forsake us. When we are discouraged, depressed, overwhelmed with confusion and self-doubt, we can look to Jesus, our refuge, and say with joy, as Paul did in Gal. 5:22: "The fruit of the Spirit is joy."

In John 1:4 we read: "And these things we write to you that your joy may be full." Many times we Christians are guilty of self-negation. In my own life at times I have belittled myself and my feeble efforts to work for the Lord. But I have also discovered that discouragement and thoughts of depression are forces that can be conquered and overcome by remembering that I am a child of God and that I truly can "rejoice in the Lord always." It is not always easy to rejoice in the Lord. Satan is often quick to try to discourage, confuse, and make us feel alone. We are not alone! Our Savior, Jesus Christ, still speaks to us through Mt. 28:20b: "…lo, I am with you always, even to the end of the age."

Again, let us consider 1 John 1:4: "…these things I write to you that your joy may be full." Perhaps the major point of all is that when we truly seek to live in the Spirit—meaning completely surrendered to our Lord (our thoughts and motives beneath His control), it is then that we have a fellowship with Him that empowers our lives and truly leads us to rejoice in the Lord and the power of His might. Perhaps it can best be summed up in the words of Christ Himself: "If you abide in Me, and My words abide in you." This leads to God-given joy through His Holy Spirit. Really, it all points to an outstanding biblical truth: Jesus is the Lord of our lives and He is our joy. This is what we sing about at Christmas: "Joy to the world; the Lord has come!" Is this joy in our hearts—if not, why not?

In John 15:11 we find: "These things I have spoken to you; that *My joy* may remain in you, and that your joy may be full." Again, in John

17:13: "...these things I speak in the world that they may have My joy fulfilled in themselves." In Neh. 8:10 joy is promised to believers: "...for this day is Holy to our Lord: do not sorrow; for the *joy* of the Lord is your strength." Ps. 16:11: "...in Your presence is fullness of joy." Ps. 30:5: "Weeping may endure for a night, but joy comes in the morning." John 16:24: "...ask, and you will receive, that your joy may be full." Rom. 14:17: "For the kingdom of God is not eating and drinking, but righteousness, and peace and *joy* in the Holy Spirit."

This last quotation leads us to discuss the third fruit or result of the Spirit—peace. Gal. 5:22 states that "the fruit of the Spirit is...peace." Peace is a gift from God that we can possess as a result of His presence in our hearts. There is a wonderful hymn which declares that peace is a wonderful gift of God's love. The Scriptures testify to this fact. The way that the word, peace, is used in our text suggests that peace is a result of spiritual development, growth, or maturity. Its use also implies that believers must work with God's Spirit to produce peace. In Rom. 14:19 we are told to "follow things that make for peace." In Gal. 5:15-21 Paul described things that war against the Spirit. In Verse 16 he urged the Galatians to "walk in the Spirit, and you shall not fulfill the lust of the flesh." There are many reasons to walk in the Spirit, and surely a major one is that we may have the peace of God in our hearts and lives. In most of Paul's letters he very early invoked that "Grace and peace from God our Father and the Lord Jesus Christ" be with those to whom he was writing. This appears in Rom. 1:7, 1 Cor. 1:2, 2 Cor. 1:2, Gal. 1:2, Eph. 1:2, Col. 1:2, 1 Thess. 1:1, 2 Thess. 1:2, 1 Tim. 1:2, 2 Tim. 1:2, Titus 1:4, and Philem. 1:3. Notice also that Paul linked the two together—grace and peace. It is because of God's grace that we can have peace with God and with ourselves. Eph. 2:14 says: For He Himself (Christ) is our peace." Phil. 4:7 tells us: "The peace of God, which surpasses all understanding will guard your hearts and minds through Christ Jesus."

Col. 3:15: "And let the peace of God rule in your hearts." 1 Thess. 5:13 tells us: "Be at peace among yourselves." 2 Thess. 3:16 states: "May the Lord of peace Himself give you peace always in every way. The Lord be with you all."

Jesus went to the cross that we might have spiritual and mental peace. John 14:27 gives us Christ's own words on this subject: "Peace I leave with you, My peace I give to you; not as the world gives do I give to you. Let not your heart be troubled, neither let it be afraid." This peace is an inward calmness and strength that is a result of Christ's presence within our hearts and minds. It is also something that increases in power as we grow toward spiritual maturity. It is a result of guidance and leadership by the Holy Spirit. God's people can afford to seek and claim spiritual serenity because it is a gift from Him through Jesus Christ our Lord.

Thus far in this message we have considered *love, joy,* and *peace* as fruits of the Spirit. We should keep in mind, however, that there are those forces that war against the presence of God's Spirit. We referred to them earlier in this message. Paul called them the "works of the flesh," and he listed some of them in Gal. 5:19-21. In other words, "walking in the Spirit" is not drifting along in and out of unconfessed sin. These fruits of the Spirit are God's free gifts to you and me; but they are not cheap. Christ paid the price for them on the cross at Calvary.

Let us turn our attention to the fourth fruit of the Spirit as found in our text: "The fruit of the Spirit is...longsuffering." In this life we want other people to do and say certain things. We have loved ones whom we tell to be, say, and do various things. We urge friends, fellow believers, and those near and dear to us to take certain courses of action. And when others do not say or do what we desire or what we have instructed them to do, we often are tempted to be impatient with them. It is then that we need the fruit of longsuffering in our minds and hearts. It is then that we need to remember and observe that first fruit of the Spirit discussed previously—love. Love suffers long according to 1 Cor. 13:4. In 2 Cor. 6:4 Paul mentioned longsuffering as one of the traits that he and other Christian workers seek to have and live before others so that their work might be more effective. In Eph. 4:1-2 Paul proclaimed to Christians: "Walk worthy of the calling with which you were called with…longsuffering, bearing with one another in love." In Col. 1:10-11 he said almost the same thing: "Walk worthy of the Lord, fully pleasing Him, being fruitful in every good work and increasing in the knowledge of God; strengthen with all might, according to His glorious power, for all patience and longsuffering with joy."

Notice that patience, love, and joy are usually mentioned in the verses of Scripture that deal with longsuffering. Longsuffering is a spiritual gift from God. It is that spiritual result (fruit) that produces endurance, patience, and strength to live in the Spirit; to witness to others; to endure misfortune or loss; to have faith, confidence, trust, and peace when it appears that God's will is hard to see or know. Longsuffering is the Christian's answer to impatience. Longsuffering is believing that God can bring good out of what appears to be a hopeless or overwhelming situation. Longsuffering is walking by faith. It is a steadfast belief that God has His own schedule for our lives and the lives of others. A longsuffering or patient person believes that God is really in control of our lives and the world. He believes that Rom. 8:28 is true: "We know that all things work together for good to those who love God, to those who are the called according to His purpose."

Longsuffering is the opposite of impatience; but it is not weakness. It is not submissive acquiescence or compliance. It is not yielding because of the constant pressure to please persons and forces that beset us. It is patience grounded in an unwavering trust that God is in charge, that God's timetable is working; not only in the universe but also in our lives.

Longsuffering and patience are qualities that were personified in Christ Jesus our Lord.

Perhaps the best way to conclude this first of two messages on the fruits of the Spirit is to say that spiritual love, joy, peace, and longsuffering are gifts that are given to believers through the work of the Holy Spirit. They are the results of being *born* of and led by the Holy Spirit. These gifts from God are not to be taken lightly. Truly, they were *purchased* through the Savior's death and resurrection. They are to be lived by believers who look to Jesus, the author and finisher of their faith.

Only as we walk in the Spirit can we have the fruits of the Spirit manifested in our lives. Walking in the Spirit does not contradict justification by faith alone, which is Paul's major theme in Galatians. Rather the spiritual walk is opening our hearts and lives to receive these gifts and then "to walk *worthy* of the calling with which you were called" (Eph. 4:1). Eph. 4:2-3 tells us how we can do this: "With all lowliness and gentleness, with longsuffering, bearing with one another in love, endeavoring to keep the unity of the Spirit in the bond of peace." And Eph. 4:23-24: "…be renewed in the spirit of your mind, and that you put on the new man (person) which was created according to God in true righteousness and holiness."

CHAPTER 15
FIVE OTHER FRUITS OF THE SPIRIT

SCRIPTURAL BACKGROUND: Gal. 5:22-26 and Eph. 6:10-18

TEXT: Gal. 5:22-23 "The fruit of the Spirit is...kindness, goodness, faithfulness,

Our text, as stated above, is a continuation of the listing of the fruits of the Spirit that we considered in the first message on fruits or results of the Spirit. In this message we want to stress some of the many truths the Holy Scriptures say about kindness, goodness, faithfulness, gentleness, and self-control. In Gal. 5:16 Paul stated: "Walk in the Spirit, and you shall not fulfill the lust of the flesh."

What does he mean by the words: "Walk in the Spirit"? From what he discussed in Galatians, Ephesians, Philippians, Colossians, Hebrews, Titus, and other writings, he seems to be saying the following:

1. Christ is our Savior and Lord. We are justified before God by faith alone. Justification is by faith alone. Gal. 3:24: "Therefore the law was our tutor to bring us to Christ, that we might be justified by faith." Gal. 3:26 states it again: "For

you are all sons of God through faith in Christ Jesus."

2. We are to "walk in the Spirit," and we are to "walk worthy of the calling" we have in Christ. Eph. 4:1 and 5:8: "For you were once in darkness, but now you are light in the Lord. Walk as children of light."

3. As we live our lives—walking in the Spirit—the Spirit of God will lead, comfort, sustain, and produce in our hearts specific fruits or results. Ephesians states several of these which are also recorded more fully in Gal. 5:22-23.

4. These fruits of the Spirit or results of the Spirit-walk are to be characteristics of the believers who are "looking unto Jesus, the author and finisher of our faith" (Heb. 12:2a). Col. 2:6-7 states: "As you therefore have received Christ Jesus the Lord, so walk in Him, rooted and built up in Him and established in the faith, as you have been taught, abounding in it with thanksgiving."

Having said this, let us move on with our study of the fruits—results—of the Spirit of God working in our lives. Kindness is the fifth fruit of the Spirit, according to our text: "The fruit of the Spirit is… kindness." In secular terms kindness is having a good or benevolent nature or disposition. The Scriptures do not contradict this definition, but the spiritual meaning goes beyond this secular meaning. Spiritual kindness is a manifestation of God's presence being shown in the lives of believers. It truly involves being led by Christ's Spirit. Kindness is God's love being set forth first in our hearts and minds; then being shown to others as gentleness, compassion, an attitude of caring, and a willingness to do good when and where we can.

Kindness is more than skin deep. True kindness comes from a spirit-filled heart. It is real and it comes to life as a deep-seated characteristic of the person who walks in the Spirit (led by the Spirit). Kindness

Does God Care about You and Me?

shows Christ living in a person. It is a form of sincere, steadfast, Christ-centered love being shown to others. It definitely is a form of mercy and caring. In the Bible mercy, love, and kindness are sometimes used interchangeably. In Col. 3:12 we are told to put on kindness: "Therefore as the elect of God, holy and beloved, put on tender mercies, kindness, humility, meekness, longsuffering; bearing with one another, and forgiving one another." The Holy Spirit can and does give us the power to be persons of kindness, and the Spirit can supply us with the power and concern to show kindness to others—in our homes, places of worship, schools, in our work, and in every aspect of our lives. Kindness is a gift of the Spirit; but it is our responsibility to grow, develop, and show kindness to others. Kindness in our hearts should be reflected in Christian living.

The apostle Paul had much to say about kindness. He evidently considered it a Godly virtue that could and did promote love and unity among Christian believers in the early church. He felt that kindness prevented cruelty and evil among believers. In Eph. 4:31-32 he wrote: "Let all bitterness, wrath, anger, clamor, and evil-speaking be put away from you, with all malice. And be kind to one another, tenderhearted, forgiving one another, even as God in Christ forgave you."

In this 21st century English language the words, mankind and kind, are often used by civic, political, and religious groups; and the two words are closely related. They both come from the root word, kinned. Love and kindness were often linked by Paul in his writing to early groups and churches. In Rom. 12:10 he said: "Be kindly, affectionate to one another with brotherly love, in honor giving preference to one another." A kind heart made sensitive by God's Spirit will be open to the feelings and needs of others. The person who shows kindness is merciful, loves in deeds as well as in words, and is far more effective in Christian service. The kind person blesses his own life and the lives of others because he avoids self-righteousness and conceit. He knows that if he is anything at all, it is because of God's imputed righteousness through Jesus Christ. God in His power and kindness restores us when we fail Him and others. For this we should be eternally thankful; and our thankfulness should be shown in a life of kindness toward others.

The sixth result or fruit of the Spirit as given in our text is goodness. "The fruit of the Spirit is…goodness" (Gal. 5:22). We are accustomed to using the term, goodness of God. We often hear men and women referred to as good people; and we also hear the word, good, used to describe a car, doctor, teacher, etc. Goodness, when used in a secular sense, is a simple term used to refer to an individual with good character, integrity, honesty, or uprightness.

In the spiritual realm we refer to the goodness of God, our Heavenly Father. As children some of us learned the short but meaningful blessing: "God is great; God is good; let us thank Him for our food." As Christians we speak of the goodness of God as being love, mercy, wisdom, power, kindness, and grace expressed toward mankind. We refer to our Lord as the Good Shepherd because in His love and mercy he does the following and even more: He saves us from sin. He provides for our needs—physical, mental, and spiritual. He leads us and protects us. He restores our souls when we turn to Him.

Our text says: "The fruit of the Spirit is…goodness." This clearly is something that the Spirit of the living Lord works in the hearts and minds of Christians. If we have any goodness in the sense of spiritual goodness, it is because His Spirit has been working in our hearts. It is because there has been an inner process guided and fueled by the Holy Spirit. Any goodness we have is the result of God's love and mercy working in our hearts. Goodness or righteousness has to be imputed to us by faith in our Savior. When we sincerely believe that God is love, mercy, and goodness; then we come to the realization that Christ came

Does God Care about You and Me?

and was made the propitiation for our sins and that God's Holy Spirit, the Spirit of the living God, can work inside our hearts and minds to produce goodness.

This imputed goodness of God compels and impels believers, first of all, to strive to be pure without and within and to perform good works for Christ and His kingdom. Christians are sinners saved by grace, God's grace. They are not perfect, but rather they are believers who seek to know and do His will in their lives.

At this point let us proceed to the seventh fruit of the Spirit. Gal. 5:22: "The fruit of the Spirit is…faithfulness." Faith is a gift from God. It is something that is apart from flesh and blood. Paul tells us in Heb. 11:1: "Now faith is the substance of things hoped for, the evidence of things not seen; and in Heb. 11:6: "But without faith it is impossible to please Him, for he who comes to God must believe that He is, and that He is a rewarder of those who diligently seek Him." The word, faith, is stressed here because it is that divine gift which is used by the Holy Spirit to enable us to be faithful. Faithfulness comes after we surrender our wills, lives, abilities, and that which we have to the service of our God. Faithfulness is being steadfast in love and service to our Lord. It is the fruit of the Spirit that keeps us praising, worshiping, and serving our God day by day.

We know that God is faithful and always will remain so. His entire nature is steadfastness and dependability; and it is His Spirit that leads, guides, and sustains us in faithfulness. Faithfulness is imputed by God's Spirit into our hearts and lives. Abiding in Him and living in faithfulness come about only because of the Spirit's power to convict us of sin; to show the way of praise, worship, and service—faithfulness—in our "walk in the Spirit." Faithfulness is a result of God working within us. Faithfulness implies loyalty, service, stability, dependability, and long-term devotion to our Lord—led by the Holy Spirit.

There are many references to the faithfulness of God in the Scriptures:

> I Cor. 1:9: "God is faithful, by whom you were called into the fellowship of His Son, Jesus Christ our Lord."
>
> 1 Thess. 5:24: "He who calls you is faithful."
>
> 2 Thess. 3:3: "But the Lord is faithful, who will establish you and guard you from the evil one."
>
> 2 Tim. 2:13: "If we are faithless, He remains faithful; He cannot deny Himself."
>
> Heb. 10:23: "Let us hold fast the confession of our hope without wavering, for He who promised is faithful."

God is faithful. He is merciful and He calls us to faithfulness through the Holy Spirit working within us. God calls us today to faithfulness in every aspect of our lives. Not only does He ask for our faithfulness; but He also promises us strength and that He will go with us all the way. God is always present and near to help us to be faithful.

In Eph. 6:10 Paul urged believers to "be strong in the Lord and in the power of His might." That is the Holy Spirit working within us and in our spiritual walk. Eph. 6:11 tells us to "put on the whole armor of God that you may be able to stand against the wiles of the devil." In Verse 13 of the same chapter Paul said: "Take up the whole armor of God"; then in Verses 14, 15, and 16 he stated exactly what that armor is:

1. Truth.
2. Righteousness—the imputed righteousness of God in Christ Jesus.

3. The gospel of peace—the peace of God; the peace we have in Christ Jesus.
4. The shield of faith—the gift of God which is in Christ Jesus.

The eighth fruit of the Spirit is gentleness. What is gentleness? Webster's dictionary states that it means "kindly, amiable, mild, not severe or rough, or violent." It also defines gentleness as "characteristic of good birth or family; well born, honorable, respected, refined, and to make gentle." Hopefully, your mind has raced ahead of these printed words, and you have sensed that in the spiritual realm, gentleness means we are of noble birth—born of the Holy Spirit. Christians are to remember that they are members of the family of God, children of God through Jesus Christ our Lord. 1 John 3:1 states: "Behold what manner of love the Father has bestowed on us, that we should be called the children of God."

In our text, Gal. 5:23, Paul said: "The fruit of the Spirit is… gentleness." What does this mean? In Christians it means strength and power, the strength and power of the Holy Spirit. It takes great strength to resist temptation, ungodliness, or all of what Paul referred to in Gal. 5:19-21 as "works of the flesh."

God-given gentleness on the part of a believer is, first of all, believing and trusting in Jesus Christ as Savior and Lord of his life. Psychologists tell us that within every normal human being there is the desire to be somebody, somebody loved and respected by others. Christ in His gentleness toward us says: "You are somebody. You are someone whom I love and have loved, and I went to Calvary for you. All that I ask of you now is that you accept Me as Savior and Lord of your life. In return for your acceptance of My offer of salvation and sonship I offer you gentleness."

The fruit of the Spirit, gentleness, tells us that we are loved and are free to be His devoted followers and stewards of His wonderful and magnificent grace. This spiritual gift of gentleness should lead us to be willing to live for our Savior, yes; but also to remember to love, help, seek, and treat others as God has forgiven and treats us. A person rooted and grounded in the faith is not afraid to be gentle toward others—regardless of race, creed, social, or political standing. Gentle Christian believers do not act selfishly or lord it over others with whom they are working or associated.

God is consistently kind and gentle toward us today and in every age. He is with us though all else fail about us. In good times and in tragedy or trouble He is with us. This is the assurance and encouragement that we get from the Holy Spirit as the fruit of gentleness is imparted to us and as we work and witness to others. Is this unusual or something of which we should be amazed? No, not at all. The fruit of the Spirit—as our text states—is gentleness. Again, what does this mean? It means that as children of God, His Spirit controls and empowers us.

How then should we live? Paul says again: "Walk in the Spirit" (Gal. 5:25). In Gal. 6:1 the Holy Spirit led Paul to write: "If a man (person) is overtaken in any trespass, you who are spiritual restore such a one in a spirit of gentleness." Gentleness is something that only the Holy Spirit can put within us. We should pray for this power because gentleness is controlled spiritual power. "It is God who works in you both to will and to do for His good pleasure" (Phil. 2:13).

The ninth fruit of the Spirit given in Gal. 5:23 is self control: "The fruit of the Spirit is…self-control." Self-control, as a fruit of the Spirit, is putting restraint on one's actions, thoughts, feelings, and emotions. This is no easy matter, but Paul said it is a result of the Holy Spirit. The Greeks of Paul's day had a special word for self-control—egkrateia.

To them egkrateia meant to have the will and strength to control oneself.

The apostle Paul found this hard to accomplish at times. In Rom. 7:19 he told of his struggle to control his actions: "For the good that I will to do, I do not do; but the evil I will not to do, that I practice." In Verses 20-24 he elaborated on this inner struggle; and in Verse 25 he stated the only way that worked for him: "I thank God through Jesus Christ our Lord!" What was he saying? The fruit of self-control is the inner person being supplied with the strength to overcome mentally and physically. That strength comes as we "walk in the Spirit." Self control is a result, and it is a positive result.

Self-control is more than just watching one's temper, speech, thoughts, or actions. It is the giving of our minds, hearts, talents, wealth, and actions to our living Lord. It means being led by His Spirit. Self-control is living one's faith. It is in the words of Rom. 12:1-2 and 9 and through the power of the Holy Spirit:

Verse 1: "Present your bodies a living sacrifice, holy, acceptable to God."

Verse 2: "And do not be conformed to this world, but be transformed by the renewing of your mind that you may prove what is that good and acceptable and perfect will of God."

Verse 9: "Let love be without hypocrisy. Abhor what is evil. Cling to what is good."

Our text for this and the previous message says: "But the fruit of the Spirit is love, joy, peace, longsuffering, kindness, goodness, faithfulness, gentleness, self-control (Gal. 5:22-23). And Gal. 5:25 tells us: "If we live in the Spirit, let us also walk in the Spirit."

CHAPTER 16

CHRISTIAN STEWARDSHIP AND DIVINE PROMISES

SCRIPTURE: 2 Cor. 9:6-11

TEXT: 2 Cor. 9:8 "And God is able to make all grace abound toward you, that you, always having all sufficiency in all things, may have an abundance for every good work."

This text contains an amazing and powerful promise of God's power; and it is to Christians a message of assurance and peace. Paul was writing to the believers at Corinth. He had several purposes in doing so. He encouraged and reminded them that God's presence, peace, grace, and mercy could and would always be with them in tribulation and trouble (2 Cor. 1:4). In Chapter 3 Paul continued this theme and stated that "our sufficiency is from God" (2 Cor. 3:5b), not from ourselves. The above verses bring us back to our text: "And God is able to make all grace abound toward you, that you, always having all sufficiency in all things, may have an abundance for every good work."

These words of comfort and assurance are also promises of God's provision for Christians—then and now. They are also words that should inspire believers to think of service and giving to Christ's church and other Christian causes: The ministry of proclaiming the gospel to those near and far, helping the sick and needy, and caring for those in trouble. In fact, notice that our text gives a reason for God's blessings: "...that you, always having all sufficiency in all things, may have an abundance for every good work." God is the giver, and we are to use our time, abilities, and service for His work.

One of the first things to think about when an individual is considering the ministry of giving is the fact that all one is and has are gifts from God. Children and adults often sing the praise song: "We give thee but thine own; what e'er the gift may be; All that we have is thine alone, a trust, O Lord, from thee." *The Doxology* reaffirms this in its first line: "Praise God from whom all blessings flow."

Ps. 24:1 is very direct in stating: "The earth is the Lord's, and all its fullness, The world and those who dwell therein." In all of our blessings, sorrows, and difficulties it is important to keep this fact in our hearts and minds. By this statement the writer means that our emotions and our minds are to be focused on God, the creator and provider. This is a reasonable expectation from God. Psalm 1:3 describes the person who delights in the law of the Lord and meditates in it: "He shall be like a tree Planted by the rivers of water, That brings forth its fruit in its season, Whose leaf also shall not wither; And whatever he does shall prosper." Psalm 1:4 states: "The ungodly are not so, But are like the chaff which the wind drives away."

Now, some may say that they know people who are financially well off but have rejected God's way and His word; and in their work and living are in no way a witness or benefit for Christ and His kingdom. The point is well taken and should be considered. When the prosperity of the ungodly is examined, Psalm 73:7b tells of the writer's temptation to envy the prosperity and wealth of the wicked and his confusion as to why they are seemingly blessed in this life. It states: "They have more than heart could wish," and in Verses 8 through 16 he continues to speak of his puzzlement as to why the rich, evil, and ungodly prosper. In Verse 17 God reveals to him the explanation: "...I went into the sanctuary of God; Then I understood their end." In Verses 18 and 19 he tells just what is to happen to them: "...You cast them down to destruction. Oh, how they are brought to desolation, as in a moment!"

Many times in today's world we too wonder about why the wicked seem to prosper while many believers do not. At such times it is helpful not to judge, but rather to think of what the Scriptures have to say about stewardship. In 1 Tim. 6:10 Paul said: "For the love of money is a root of all kinds of evil, for which some have strayed from the faith in their greediness, and pierced themselves through with many sorrows." Notice that this verse of Scripture, taken from *The New King James Version*, states that the *love of money* is a root of all *kinds* of evil. This is important for study as we consider giving and Christian stewardship. In today's world money is the medium of exchange used in most business transactions and other areas of life such as giving and receiving. The word Paul used for love of money was *philarguria*. It is a compound Greek word, according to the Greek dictionary, composed of two words, *philia*, which means love and *arguria*, which means money or silver.

Someone has said that if you really want to know a person, look at the record of their use of money. How we use money for buying the things we want for ourselves, our loved ones, those sick and in need, and for the support of God's church and the spread of the gospel tells very much about who we really are. Jesus said: "...where your treasure is, there your heart will be also" (Mt. 6:21). Does this mean we are to show no concern for money, support of family, and loved ones? No, not at all, for we are to plan and save for the present and future of ourselves and our loved ones. However, when we reach the point that our saving, financial planning, and use of money for our own pleasure and satisfaction are given top priority in our minds and hearts, it is then that we have become so in love with money and material things that they take first place in our lives. God becomes second place, or less, and we miss the joy of giving and Christian stewardship.

Money does talk, and the use of it speaks volumes about ourselves and others. In Gen. 22:14 Abraham, thinking of God's provision, referred to God as *Jehovah-jireh,* the one who provides. Today He is still the provider for His people. We acknowledge Him as the good shepherd when we read or repeat "The Lord is my shepherd" (Ps. 23:1). The important thing to keep constantly in mind is that God gives to us so that we may give to those in need. Giving and doing for God's work and for others involve more than money. It also includes our time, service, and definitely our talents and abilities. Remember to whom much is given, from him much will be required (Luke 12:48b).

As we work, do financial planning, budget our money, service, and time; we must not center our love and devotion on things, bank accounts, positions, or worldly power. Instead, as we save and serve, let us trust God and seek to have faith that He will continue to provide for us and indeed, bless our efforts even more than in the past. Ask Him to replace worry and concern with faith that comes about as we work, study, and give to the church and to those in need. Our text gives us a promise on this.

If we constantly worry over money and our use of time and abilities, we can find ourselves in a state of mental and spiritual distress. The solution, the Bible says, is to "be anxious for nothing, but in everything by prayer and supplication, with thanksgiving, let your requests be made known to God; and the peace of God, which surpasses all understanding, will guard your hearts and minds through Christ Jesus" (Phil. 4:6-7). Good stewardship of God's blessings demands that we do our part in faith and efforts that God may bless us, and through our prayers and work, bless others. 1 Peter 5:7 tells us to cast "all your care upon Him, for He cares for you"; but even a casual reading of 1 Peter, Chapter 5 will show that God expects submission, prayer, and efforts on the believer's

Does God Care about You and Me?

part for a blessing to come to him. Then it is that our text becomes a comforting, blessed assurance: "And God is able to make all grace abound toward you, that you, always having all sufficiency, in all things, may have an abundance for every good work" (2 Cor. 9:8).

Malachi 3:7-8 tell of Israel's rebellion against God, their forsaking of Him, their disobedience toward Him, and their robbing of Him. In Verse 8 the prophet raises a question that strikes at the heart of their unfaithfulness: "Will a man rob God?" The question is answered in the same verse: "In tithes and offerings." In Verse 10 the people are told what they should do, and they are also given a promise: "'Bring all the tithes into the storehouse That there may be food in My house, And try Me now in this,' Says the Lord of hosts, 'if I will not open for you the windows of heaven And pour out for you such blessing That there will not be room enough to receive it.'"

In biblical times the storehouse of God meant a place where food was stored. Gen. 41:56 tells of Joseph building and storing food for the people—Egyptians and Israelites—to use during the seven years of famine. It is important to note that Joseph built storehouses in many places and stored food in them (Gen. 41:48). Verse 49 states: "Joseph gathered very much grain, as the sand of the sea, until he stopped counting, for it was immeasurable." Your writer stresses this here because it is tied in to Mal. 3:10 which teaches that following God's instructions leads to Him abundantly providing for His people.

Today many believers consider the church to be the storehouse to which they give their tithes and offerings. They do this because they feel that the church, its Bible study, missions, and ministries provide the best organization for doing God's work and for the teaching and preaching of the gospel. Other Christians who have convictions on tithing and special offerings may or may not follow the storehouse concept, but they do give to their church and other worthwhile causes. Our text, 1 Cor. 9:8, makes it clear that our giving is to be for "every good cause": "God is able to make all grace abound toward you, that you, always having all sufficiency in all things, may have an abundance for every good work." Both of the above groups also cherish 1 Cor. 16:2a: "On the first day of the week let each one of you lay something aside, storing up as he may prosper."

Christian stewardship recognizes God's ownership of all that is good. This includes our lives (Rom. 14:8) and existence, the earth and all therein (Ps. 24:1-2), our souls and minds, and all of the material possessions we own (Deut. 22:6). God gave His Son, the Christ, to purchase our redemption (1 Cor. 6:20). God has endowed us with special gifts and abilities (Luke 19:13 and Mt. 25:14-15). In turn, He expects us to be faithful (Mt. 6:33); and this faithfulness is to be done in grateful devotion (1 Pet. 4:10). We are accountable to God (Luke 12:15), and He promises to reward our faithfulness in this life, as stated in our text, and also in the next life: "For the Son of Man will come in the glory of His Father with His angels, and then He will reward each according to his works" (Mt. 16:27).

2 Cor. 9:6-11, our background Scripture for this message, and 2 Cor. 8:1-12 give valuable guidelines for Christian stewardship. Some of the most obvious ones are as follows:

> God's mercy and grace through faith make believers God's children. Thus Christians acknowledge that all they are and have are a trust from Him (1 Cor. 4:2).
>
> Christians are stewards (Luke 19:13).
>
> Christians as stewards are accountable (Rom 14:12 and 1 Pet. 4:5).
>
> Christian giving is to be sacrificial giving (2 Cor. 9:6 and 8:3).
>
> Christians are to give because they want to give—not because they are forced to give (2 Cor. 8:3 and 8:12).
>
> Christians are responsible to God for their giving and the use of their talents (2 Cor., Chapter 3 and 9:4-7).

Does God Care about You and Me?

> Christian stewardship of money, possessions, and talents should be in relation to what God has given them (2 Cor. 8:12, 1 Pet. 4:10).
>
> Christians are to be steadfast, constant, and systematic in their stewardship (2 Cor. 9:6-12).
>
> Christians should give, serve, and minister to the Lord according to their personal convictions and decisions (2 Cor. 9:7-8).
>
> Christians should serve and give with a very positive mental attitude—not grudgingly (2 Cor. 9:7-8).

Jesus, the Christ, wants us to grow spiritually and in every area of our lives. It is His desire that we grow in Christian graces, patience, kindness, love, and concern for others. It is this writer's belief that giving according to the guidelines stated above will bring joy and blessedness to the giver. God invested in us by giving His Son for us. Our lives, talents, abilities, and possessions are truly gifts from Him. 2 Cor. 9:8 confirms this and also gives a promise: "And God is able to make all grace abound toward you; that you, always having all sufficiency in all things, may have an abundance for every good work."

2 Cor. 8:1-7 speaks of the grace of God and also brings out that until an individual is giving in response to God's grace, until it is done in response to all God has provided, he will not experience true joy in giving. Christian stewardship means aligning one's life with God's grace and will. Sowing generously leads to generous reaping. Does this mean it is the way to become rich? Not at all; but it does mean that God has promised to provide for a person's needs when it is essential: "...that you, always having all sufficiency in all things, may have an abundance for every good work" (2 Cor. 9:8b). Christians are to be stewards of their blessings and resources.

God wants us to grow in His grace and in His word and to mature in discipleship. A large part of that is growing in Christian stewardship. Stewardship of our blessings is linked very closely to other Christian virtues: Grace, patience, kindness, knowledge, spiritual boldness, and, yes, growth in giving of ourselves and our possessions: "God is able to make all grace abound toward you" (2 Cor. 9:8a).

Giving to God's church and Christian causes shows how we measure our love and devotion to Christ's church and its work. Some feel that the church is always asking members to give. This is true and is the way it should be if the church is always reaching out in its ministry to fellow Christians, the sick and suffering, people in need, and the unsaved. These are areas that require giving on the part of believers. Jesus said in Luke 12:34: "For where your treasure is, there your heart will be also." Mt. 6:20 tells believers to "lay up for yourselves treasures in heaven." The only way this can be done is by investing in Christ's work and in the spiritual lives of others.

In a previous century there was a man named S. D. Phelps. He was a highly educated person with a Doctorate of Divinity. He believed that people were created to work and to use their minds for Christ and His church. He wrote a poem in 1899 that later Robert Lowry set to music. It acknowledges that Phelps was thinking of God's blessings and the fact that they are for a purpose:

"Savior, Thy dying love Thou gavest me,
Nor should I aught withhold, Dear Lord, from Thee:
In love my soul would bow, My heart fulfill its vow,
Some offering bring Thee now, Something for Thee."

The text, 2 Cor. 9:8 gives a promise—a Divine promise—concerning giving and the use of what God has given to Christians: "And God is able to make all grace abound toward you, that you, always having all sufficiency in all things, have an abundance for every good work."

CHAPTER 17

THE RESURRECTION OF JESUS CHRIST—AN EASTER MESSAGE

SCRIPTURAL BACKGROUND: 1 Cor. 15:1-23; 1 Pet. 1:3-5; John 11:25-26

TEXT: Acts 1:3: "…He also presented Himself alive after His suffering by many infallible proofs, being seen by them during forty days and speaking of the things pertaining to the kingdom of God."

The first four verses of 1 Corinthians 15 contain a summary of the gospel of Jesus Christ. In those four verses the apostle Paul set forth the basics of the Christian's hope for eternal life. This hope is based on Christ's virgin birth, sinless life, sacrificial death on the cross, and glorious resurrection from the grave. In the very first verses of 1 Corinthians Paul declared that he was writing not only to the believers at Corinth but also "…to those who are sanctified in Christ Jesus, called to be saints (meaning set aside and called out) with all who in every place call on the name of Jesus Christ our Lord."

In verse 3b of Chapter 15 Paul said that "…Christ died for our sins according to the Scriptures"; and in Verse 4 he continued: "And that He was buried, and that He rose again the third day according to the

Scriptures." Verses 5-6 tell that "He was seen by Cephas, then by the twelve. After that He was seen by over five hundred brethren at once, of whom the greater part remain to the present, but some have fallen asleep" (in other words, they have passed away from this earth—died). Paul went on to say in Verses 7-8: "After that He was seen by James, then by all the apostles. Then last of all He was seen by me also as by one born out of that time."

As one reads on in 1 Corinthians 15, he will find that the Holy Spirit led Paul to stress the absolute necessity of the resurrection, not only of Christ, but also of all who believe in Him. In Verse 14 he stated: "And if Christ is not risen, then our preaching is empty and your faith is also empty." In other words, Paul is saying that the resurrection of Christ Jesus is a fundamental in Christian faith. He continued in Verse 15 to point out that if, indeed, Christ was not resurrected from the dead that really those who had been believing in and witnessing for Christ were false witnesses, "if...the dead do not rise." Verses 16-19 emphasize the hopelessness of a faith without the hope and assurance of Christ's victory over death and the grave. "For if the dead do not rise, then Christ is not risen. And if Christ is not risen, your faith is futile; you are still in your sins! Then also those who have fallen asleep in Christ have perished. If in this life only we have hope in Christ, we are of all men the most pitiable." In other words, without the resurrection of Christ those who believe in Him have nothing—only a false hope—a faith without proof or power.

After Paul pointed out these negative arguments, he stated the true facts of the matter by declaring in no uncertain terms that "...now Christ is risen from the dead, and has become the firstfruits of those who have fallen asleep. For since by man came death, by Man also came the resurrection of the dead. For as in Adam all die, even so in Christ all shall be made alive" (1 Cor. 15:20-23).

Does God Care about You and Me?

As many Christian writers point out, the work and life of Jesus Christ does not end with His sacrificial death on the cross and His burial in another person's tomb. The resurrection is, as stated above, fundamental to the *good news*, the Gospel. As the hymn writer, Alfred H. Ackley, wrote: "We serve a risen Savior, He's in the world today"; and Ackley continued his message of truth by asking and answering the question: "You ask me how I know He lives, He lives within my heart."

After His resurrection Jesus appeared to many different people, but as Myron S. Augsburger pointed out in his commentary: "His message was the same."[12] It was the message of the kingdom of God. The risen Lord appeared to many of His disciples over a period of 40 days. Our text, Acts 1:3, tells us:"…He also presented Himself alive after His suffering by many infallible proofs, being seen by them during forty days and speaking of the things pertaining to the kingdom of God."

To set down fully the order in which "He presented Himself alive" requires a careful study of the record given by Matthew, Mark, Luke, and John; by Luke in Acts 1:2-12; and by Paul in 1 Cor. 14:5, 7-8. Even then, biblical scholars are not sure of the exact sequence of Christ presenting Himself; but to believers there is every reason to believe in the factual, historical, and spiritual meaning of the resurrection—which is, because He lives, we will also live.

The Bible states that Christ made the following appearances:

To Mary Magdalene: John 10:11-18 and Mark 16:9

To other women as they left the garden: Mt. 28:1-10

To the disciple Peter: 1 Cor. 15:5 and Luke 24:34

To the two disciples on the Emmaus Road: Mark 16:12 and Luke 24:13-31

To ten disciples in a room in Jerusalem (Thomas was not present): John 20:19-22

To the 11 disciples (Thomas was present this time): 1 Cor. 15:5,

Mark 16:14, and John 20:24-27

To seven disciples beside the Sea of Tiberias: John 21:1-14

To the 11 disciples in Galilee: Mt. 28:16-20

To over five hundred people gathered together: 1 Cor. 15:7

To James: 1 Cor. 15:7

To the 11 disciples: 1 Cor. 15:7, Luke 24:36-40, and Acts 1:3-11

To the apostle Paul (called Saul at that time) on the Damascus Road: 1 Cor. 15:8

A study of the gospels shows that there are some "variations in the recorded sequences of the times Jesus appeared to believers after His resurrection." This, according to Augsburger, in no way "discredits" the truth and factual accounts of Jesus' resurrection.[13] Instead, they highlight the importance of the individual and *authentic character* of the various individuals and groups who actually witnessed the appearances of the risen Lord. The early believers who saw the resurrected Christ looked upon His resurrection as a God-given fulfillment of His promises and message. They were not concerned with *their* importance; they were moved and rejoiced that God had raised up their Savior and Master. To them it was not so important that something magnificent had happened to them; but rather that Jesus was alive and as our text states: "…He also presented Himself alive after His suffering by many *infallible* proofs, being seen by them during forty days and speaking of the things pertaining to the kingdom of God" (Acts 1:3).

To the disciples the resurrection was the miraculous event that had happened to Christ; and it was also the power of that resurrection and the coming of the Holy Spirit that empowered them to set forth—even in the face of great hardships, dangers, and death—to bear witness of His resurrection and message. They knew it was a reality. During the time

Does God Care about You and Me?

between the crucifixion and resurrection of Jesus, the disciples were overwhelmed and frightened by the events. They were living with the reality of Christ's death and with what they then thought was a lost faith and hopeless dream. The resurrection and His appearances changed these followers of Jesus. Mary Magdalene carried the message of an empty tomb to the disciples. Simon Peter and John, "the other disciple whom Jesus loved," ran to the tomb and saw that Christ was not there. John, "…who came to the tomb first, went in also, and he saw and believed" (John 10:4). The other disciples saw and believed, and their fear and discouragement changed after they had experienced the reality and power of Christ's resurrection, and after they had received the Holy Spirit. Acts 1:3, our text, states that Christ "…presented Himself alive after His suffering by many infallible proofs, being seen by them during forty days and speaking of the things pertaining to the kingdom of God."

Even the apostle Thomas, who at first was very doubtful of the resurrection message, shed his skepticism when confronted by the risen Lord. He had said: "Unless I see in His hands the print of the nails, and put my hand into His side, I will not believe" (John 20:25b). However, eight days later the disciples who were "…again inside, and Thomas with them, Jesus came, the doors being shut, and stood in the midst, and said, 'Peace to you!' Then He said to Thomas, 'Reach your finger here, and look at My hands, and reach your hand here, and put it into My side. Do not be unbelieving, but believing'" (John 20:26b-27). Thomas' answer was one we must give as he did: "My Lord and my God" (John 20:28b).

There is another great message of truth here in regard to the so-called "doubting Thomas." That truth might cause some to be distressed; yet, it should and does cause the believer to rejoice. The message is this: Christ knew Thomas; eight days before this appearance He knew about Thomas' statement that he would not believe unless he had proof. Jesus saw and heard it. Our Savior and Lord sees and hears us today just as

He saw and heard Thomas. Thus this is the message for us: Jesus knows our every weakness as well as our strengths and needs. Truly, "His eye is on the sparrow," and we have every spiritual reason to believe in Him and to trust Him fully.

There is more for us to consider in the words Jesus spoke to Thomas on that occasion: "Thomas, because you have seen me, you have believed. Blessed are those who have not seen and yet have believed" (John 20:29). Today, by faith, we believe in Jesus Christ because of His word and His works. John 20:30-31 tells us: "And truly Jesus did many other signs in the presence of His disciples which are not written in the book; but these are written that you may believe that Jesus is the Christ, the Son of God, and that believing you may have life in His name." His word we accept as truth; His death we accept by His word and by our faith in His promises; His resurrection we accept and believe according to His word, His promises, and His appearances; and as Luke tells us in Acts 1:3b: "…by many infallible proofs, being seen by them (the apostles) during forty days and speaking of the things pertaining to the kingdom of God."

Matthew in his gospel spoke of the women who on the first day of the week, even before daybreak, came to the tomb; and in Mt. 28:1-10 he stated that there was an earthquake; an angel of the Lord appeared, rolled away the huge stone; and those present—the guards—shook from fear," and "became like dead men." Barclay says that it is appropriate that the two Marys should be the first ones to hear the angel tell of the risen Savior and Lord, and indeed the first to see and hear the risen Lord.[14] They were also the first to be able to proclaim the good news of the resurrection: "…Jesus met them, saying: 'Rejoice! ….Do not be afraid. Go and tell My brethren to go to Galilee, and there they will see Me'" (Mt. 28:9-10).

These two women had been very close and faithful to Jesus. They were present when He died on the cross; when others ran away, they did not; when He was laid in Joseph's tomb, they were there; and they were the first to know the powerful truth of the resurrection: "He is not here; for He is risen, *as He said*. Come see the place where the Lord lay" (Mt. 28:6). The angel of the Lord urged them to believe and pointed out that Christ's resurrection was exactly as He had promised and said it would be. In other words, the angel was saying to them: "Believe His promises and the words He has spoken." They did, and we are to do the same today.

The many and varied appearances of Jesus after His resurrection were considered by Luke as infallible proofs of His victory over sin, death, and the grave (Acts 1:3). The reaction of the disciples to His resurrection is also another proof of His victory over death and sin. Their reaction to His glorious resurrection was one of joy, courage, reassurance, and a sound belief. Barclay, writing about the loyalty, joy, and belief of the two Marys who first saw the resurrected Lord states that there were three major *imperatives* they felt they must carry out.[15] These were as follows:

> They were to believe and not fear. The angels and the resurrected Christ stressed this to them.
>
> They were to share the good news as the angel of the Lord and Christ Himself told them to do. The angel said to them: "Go quickly and tell His disciples that He is risen from the dead. He is going before you into Galilee" (Mt. 28:7). But before they reached the disciples, Jesus met them and told them to rejoice and not to be afraid, but to "…Go and tell My brethren to go to Galilee and there they will see me" (Mt. 28:9b-10). They were to tell them of Christ's resurrection and to proclaim it to others.
>
> These two women were to rejoice. Then, and indeed in our day, persons who have met the Lord and experienced His sacred

> presence rejoice because they have a risen Savior who truly is alive and lives within their hearts.

In the last meeting with His disciples Jesus spoke three things that are of great importance to believers today. He assured them of His absolute power. Matthew put it this way: "And Jesus came and spoke to them, saying, 'all authority has been given to me in heaven and on earth'" (Mt. 28:18). Then Jesus set forth what we know today as the Great Commission: "Go therefore and make disciples of all the nations; and…teach them to observe all things that I have commanded you" (Mt. 28:19-20a). Then Christ said: "…And lo, I am with you always, even to the end of the age" (Mt. 28:20b). This is Christ's powerful promise of His presence.

The appearances of Jesus, His words to His disciples, and the coming of the Holy Spirit turned these individuals around and empowered them. Before, they had feared, fled, and distanced themselves from their former Master. They had forgotten His teachings to them, the necessity of His suffering, and the absolute promise of His resurrection. Now, however, they had seen and experienced the presence and power of Christ, the resurrected Lord, for themselves. Now they were no longer downcast, disillusioned, and afraid. They now knew they were to serve a living Savior. Jesus had preached the kingdom of God before His death on the cross. After His resurrection His preaching and teaching centered on the same message of God's kingdom. Now these eleven and the other believers were to proclaim that message. They were to wait for the coming of the Holy Spirit, after which, they would go out with renewed faith and power. As a result, the Roman and Greek worlds were changed.

Today God's Holy word says to you and me that He is our Savior and Lord. Whosoever will may come to this risen Savior who has power to save any and all who will believe on His name; a Savior who can forgive our sins and failures; who through the power of His blood and the Holy

Spirit can empower us to live and serve in His kingdom; a Savior and Lord who has been victorious over death and the grave and who has said: "Let not your heart be troubled; you believe in God, believe also in me. In My Father's house are many mansions; if it were not so, I would have told you. I go to prepare a place for you; and if I go and prepare a place for you, I will come again and receive you to Myself; that where I am, there you may be also" (John 14:1-3). He is the risen Lord who said to His disciples—and who speaks to us today: "...because I live, you will live also" (John 14:19).

Peter and John received the message of the empty tomb from the women who had already seen the risen Lord, but they ran to see it for themselves. This was something they needed to experience first-hand. John 20:4-8 tells us: "So they both ran together, and the other disciple (John) outran Peter and came to the tomb first...yet he did not go in. Then Simon Peter came, following him, and went into the tomb; and he saw the linen cloths lying there.... Then the other disciple, who came to the tomb first, went in also; and he saw and believed." Today by faith and belief in Christ Jesus we can experience the New Birth and the resurrection in our hearts and in our minds.

CHAPTER 18

AFFIRMATION—ENCOURAGEMENT—OF OURSELVES AND OTHERS

SCRIPTURAL BACKGROUND: Acts 9:1-20 and 1 John 3:1-2

TEXT: 1 John 3:1a: "Behold what manner of love the Father has bestowed on us that we should be called children of God."

The word affirmation comes from the word affirm. Affirm means to state or assert positively. It also means to maintain, endorse, encourage, accept, and believe something as true; to assert solemnly. Thus the word affirmation is the act of affirming. In this message my major purpose is to state that I believe Christians are children of God and that, as His children, we have reason to believe in ourselves and other Christians. But we constantly need to affirm ourselves and others—especially other Christians. In 1 John 3:1a we read: "Behold what manner of love the Father has bestowed on us that we should be called children of God"; and in 1 John 3:2: "Beloved, now we are children of God; and it has not yet been revealed what we shall be, but we know that when He is revealed, we shall be like Him, for we shall see Him as He is."

The point I want to make is that as children of God we should affirm and encourage ourselves and other Christians whether they are family members, friends, or others with whom we have contact. There are many examples of individuals and groups in the Bible encouraging one another. In the next few pages I want to deal with some instances where individuals affirmed and encouraged others in ways that resulted in important benefits to the lives of those affirmed and those giving the affirmation.

One of the most spectacular instances is found in Acts 9:1-19. It involves Paul and Ananias and their "God arranged" meeting in Damascus after Paul's vision. The vision was a miracle, but there were two other miracles involved. Lloyd John Ogilvie wrote about them in his book, *Silent Strength for My Life*.[16] Ananias, according to Ogilvie, received a miracle before helping to perform one. Ananias knew about the terrible Pharisee called Saul of Tarsus. He knew about the death of Stephen with Saul standing by, and that Saul "made havoc of the church, entering every house, and dragging off men and women, committing them to prison" (Acts 8:3). He knew that Saul, "breathing threats and murder against the disciples of the Lord," had received permission from the high priest "that if he found any who were of the Way (Christian believers) whether men or women, he might bring them bound to Jerusalem" (Acts 9:1-2). God spoke to Ananias: "The Lord said to him, 'Go for he (Saul) is a chosen vessel of Mine to bear My name before Gentiles, kings, and the children of Israel.' ...and Ananias went" (Acts 9:15-17a).

Here we have the first of the two miracles I would have you to consider. Ananias' fear and, indeed, hatred of Saul had been transformed into loving affirmation of the future minister to Jews and Gentiles. This had to take place before Ananias could lay loving, God-empowered hands on Saul and say: "Brother Saul, the Lord Jesus, who appeared to you on the road as you came, has sent me" (Acts 9:17b). Thus God, using and affirming Ananias, produced a true miracle in him in that his fear and concern were changed to obedient, trusting, Divine service to Saul who would be an apostle to witness to Jews and especially Gentiles.[17] Think of it! Saul was probably the most active enemy of the early church before his conversion and Ananias' mission to him. So Ananias had to obey God's voice—overcoming his hate and fear of Saul—so that the Lord could use him to bring His healing, reconciliation, and love to Saul.

Saul had hurt and even killed believers—he was then Ananias' and Christians' worst enemy, but God knew what could be done by him once he was converted. God had spoken to Saul and God spoke to Ananias. Ananias affirmed Saul as to what had happened to him on the Damascus road. Ananias was affirmed in that God spoke to him and used him to convert, baptize, and help Saul get started on his mission.

Now the point of the above for us is to think of who we need to affirm and encourage today, this week, this year, or in our lifetimes. Are there family members, friends, and others who need our encouragement and help—now? There may even be those who have been or really are our enemies; yet we, as Ananias, are charged to do what we can for whomever we can—to affirm and encourage them. God commanded Ananias; He still commands today. God told him: "Go (to Saul), for he is a chosen vessel of Mine to bear My name before Gentiles…," and he went. He had to "trust and obey." Doubtless there was more said between him and the Lord than is given in the book of Acts, but enough is given for us to know and learn from the miracle that took place in Ananias' mind and heart. We, like him, must be willing to forgive our enemies and other persons we may not like so that God can use us.

Saul had been praying. In addition, notice the second miracle: *Saul trusted Christ, was baptized, and his sight was restored.* No doubt, he knew something about the teachings of Jesus even while he was persecuting believers; but surely God, using the vision Saul had and the teaching and baptizing by Ananias, worked a great and lasting miracle in his conversion and acceptance of the call from God to be an apostle. Saul, whose name was changed to Paul, said in his own words: "I was not disobedient to the heavenly vision." God used Ananias; He affirmed him and then, using him, God affirmed Saul. *Saul became Paul,* the great, powerful, militant missionary to the Gentiles and thousands of Jews (See the book of Hebrews in the New Testament).

I know of many instances when members of my and my wife's family, teachers, and friends took some action to help (affirm) me, thus encouraging me to accomplish objectives important to me, my family, and work I was trying to do for the Lord and others. Is there someone you know who needs to be affirmed today by the risen Lord using you? How? It could be by phone, a visit, a letter, a word of encouragement, by e-mail, etc. Let them know you believe in them, that you pray for them, and that God is available—a friend that is closer than a brother. "Lo, I am with you always even to the end of the world!" In my own life during times of opportunity, sickness, success, challenge, indecision, self-doubt, and loneliness God has given me affirmation through His word, His presence, prayer, family members, and Christian friends. These strong factors have helped me to overcome self-doubt, fear, and uncertainty.

God reaffirms us in His words as given in Mt. 5:13-14: "You are the salt of the earth.... You are the light of the world." Paul said, "Christ in you, the Hope of Glory." It is important to have affirmation from Christian friends and relatives. It is all the more important and liberating to hear it from the Lord and His word. He believes in us; He died and rose from the dead for us and has promised never to leave us alone. Paul stated: "My God will supply all your needs through Christ Jesus our Lord." God knows us. He knows what we have been, what we are by His grace, and what we can be and do when our lives are yielded to Him and we are committed to service in His kingdom. We need Him; His kingdom needs us.

He is a friend who will never leave nor forsake us. In Heb. 13:5b-6 we read: "For He Himself has said, 'I will never leave you nor forsake you.' So we may boldly say: 'The Lord is my helper, I will not fear'." This is the height of affirmation. How many earthly friends who would or could say that do we have? How many relatives and friends who would count on you or me for such affirmation do we have? Many times we are afraid to get very close with friends or to let them get too close to us. A true Christian friend is one we can trust and who can count on us; one with whom we do not have to put up fronts or pretense. We can be authentic with them and they can with us.

Jesus Christ knows all about us, and He has promised never to go away. We can know Him in close friendship through His word, prayers, service, and in living for others as well as ourselves. He offers His affirmation constantly. He stands at the door and knocks. We must open for Him and for others. He is a true friend who knows all about us, but still affirms us and will not leave us alone. We must, as Ananias and Paul did, follow His commands.

We can affirm others and ourselves by truly listening to them—listening carefully and respectfully until we actually hear and understand what they are trying to tell us. In Prov. 18:13 we read: "He who answers a matter before he hears it, it is folly."

When I taught educational psychology, the psychologists had a term for listening but not really hearing or understanding. It was "cognitive dissonance."[18] Often I found teachers *and* students guilty of this. It means that a person appears to be listening and the speaker thinks the person is listening, but in reality he is not; thus there is no true communication. This is because the speaker is saying one thing and the hearer is thinking of something else. The result is miscommunication. Husbands and wives, clergy and believers, friends and relatives, and even God and man have problems in communication.[19]

So what is God saying to us in Prov. 18:13? I believe He is saying: "Listen carefully, make sure you understand and have heard correctly. Get the message the speaker is trying to tell you; and in doing so, you will affirm the speaker and yourself. Be patient, especially if it is a child, a young person, a student, or a friend." Many, many times as a counselor, teacher, minister, husband, friend, parent, and grandfather I have seen this happen. As Christians we must listen carefully to our inner minds and to others. Others may be hurting, rejoicing, or somewhere in between these extremes. Our job is to make sure we let the other child of God communicate affirmation.[20] Yes, it is true that some friends and loved ones may try our patience, but we as Christians must try to listen patiently and understand the message. Sometimes loved ones and others say to us: "You were not listening." Unfortunately, often they are correct. Listening is vital as we attempt to serve our Lord, work with others, and try to reaffirm those who need affirmation. There surely will be times when we may have to ask the person speaking to repeat what was said, or we may say: "As I listened, I thought this is what you were telling me. Am I right?"

We need to be active listeners. By this I mean we not only are quiet and listening patiently, but also we empathize with the person speaking and silently pray that we can in some very positive way be used by our Lord to encourage, help, and affirm the speaker ourselves.[21] In our attempts to listen to others we surely must remember the third Beatitude: "Blessed are the meek, for they shall inherit the earth." The Hebrew word for meek is *anaw*. It does not mean weakness. It means one who is teachable, moldable, leadable, who will not only listen to God's word and respond but also knows that God is our strength and in Him we can overcome. It is knowing that God can and wants to affirm each one of us.[22]

Consider the case of Archippus. Col. 4:17 tells about him: "And say to Archippus, 'Take heed to the ministry which you have received in the Lord, that you may fulfill it'." Archippus was an outstanding minister of the gospel and a faithful member and officer in the church at Colosse. Paul, in his letter to the Colossians, encouraged Archippus—he sent his affirmation to him. Paul's words to him can be applied to us today. We need to get on with what God has led us to see as our calling—our service for the Lord. We constantly need to be seeking and expressing God's plan for our lives and His service. There is a ministry appointed for you and me.

In other words, let us be faithful to do what we can, where and when we can. We are to seek His leadership and the strength He will supply. We are to care for and minister to people. In this way, "as we do His good will," we find our own place of service. Have you thought about it in that way? All of us are unique, and God has an individual plan for each one. As we serve Him and others, he affirms—encourages—and strengthens us. Let us not say, "I can't do very much" or "if I were as smart as so and so, I would serve." God says, "I will be with you," and His strength will be sufficient for you. The Psalmist wrote in Ps. 73:26b: "God is the strength of my heart and my portion forever." Only God can design and guide us in living His individual plan for us. We can find that special plan of service by trusting and obeying as He leads.

Think for a moment of Lydia in Acts 16:14: "Now a certain woman named Lydia heard us. She was a seller of purple from the city of Thyatira, who worshipped God. The Lord opened her heart to heed the things spoken by Paul." In other words, God spoke to Lydia and opened her heart. God affirmed His presence, and Lydia believed the message Paul was preaching. Verse 16:15 tells us that "when she and her household were baptized, she begged us, saying, 'If you have judged me to be faithful to the Lord, come to my house and stay.' So she persuaded us." Thus we see Lydia was affirmed by God; Paul was affirmed by her and her faithfulness.

Lydia was an outstanding business woman. She was also a spiritual leader for a group who met to worship God. This was taking place in a country ruled by Romans. After her conversion she became a spiritual leader in the church at Philippi. It was the Lord who opened her heart to the gospel and to service. Her conversion was a miracle. When we walk in *His way, God affirms* us and there is rejoicing in Heaven.

Let us consider Barnabas, whose name means "Son of Encouragement." The book of Acts mentions him several times, and in each case he is acting to give others God-like encouragement. Always he was encouraging people and the church. He encouraged and was a friend to Paul and a fellow missionary with him. Even after Mark was a missionary dropout, Barnabas cared for him and helped him to become an outstanding leader in the early church. Barnabas stands out in early church history because of the encouragement he gave to others that led them to make contributions to God's work and God's early church. *How much today do we need persons who encourage, who build up others, who infuse hope, who are used by God to encourage others! Who do you need to contact—by phone, letter, e-mail, or personal visit?* All of the above and numerous other individuals recorded in Scripture show that people can change when affirmed by a Godly person and the Holy Spirit.

In the past as a speech coach, basketball and baseball coach, supervisor of student teachers, pastor of churches, college counselor, and teacher; I have been amazed at what others can do when they are affirmed, encouraged, believed "in." I am also amazed at the things that can be accomplished not only in others, but also in ourselves when we, like Barnabas, have a Christ-filled attitude toward ourselves and others. There are many examples of individuals encouraging and affirming others; in other words, showing trust and belief in them as children of God and believing in them as Christians.

We never outgrow our need for affirmation. Perhaps one of the best examples comes from Jesus in the Beatitudes and the Sermon on the Mount. The word, blessed, in Hebrew means cherished, called out, happy, a special person. As someone has appropriately said, "Most of us know about our sins, failures, defeats. What we need is to know that someone cares and believes in us."

When Jesus was baptized, God's voice was heard to say: "This is my beloved Son in whom I am well pleased." We are made children of God through our faith, belief, and conversion in Christ. Thus God has affirmed us as His children through the New Birth. Can God say of us: "This is my beloved child in whom I am well pleased"? Do we need more encouragement? At times, yes. It is available in God's word, prayer, and the fellowship of Christian friends. Christ affirmed the women at the empty tomb, the two disciples walking on the road, the disciple Thomas, the disciples all together, and many others.

Our text—John 3:1a—tells of God's affirmation for us; however, Christ wants you and me to practice this as part of our ministry to others. This is something most of us can do. Affirmation of people and family can be a vital part of witnessing.

Endnotes

1. Lloyd John Ogilvie, *Silent Strength for My Life*, Eugene, Ore.: Harvest House Publishers, 1990, pp. 31-32.
2. Billy Graham, *Hope for Each Day*, Nashville, Tn.: J. Countryman, a division of Thomas Nelson, Inc., 2002, pp. 128, 131, 160, and other pages.
3. Ogilvie, *Ibid.*, p. 221.
4. *Ibid.*
5. Lloyd John Ogilvie, *Silent strength for My Life*, Eugene, Or: Harvest House Publishers, 1990, p. 349.
6. *Ibid.*, p. 379. (Used by permission)
7. Frank Charles Thompson, *The New Chain-Reference Bible*, 3rd ed., Indianapolis: B. B. Kirkbridge Bible Co., 1934, "Analyses of Books," p. 223.
8. George Keith, "How Firm a Foundation," in *Make Christ King Combined*, Chicago: The Glad Tidings Company, 1916, p. 188.
9. Jessie Brown Pounds, "The Way of the Cross," *Ibid.*, p. 6.
10. Charles Wesley, "Blessed Be the Name of the Lord," *Ibid.*, p. 262.
11. Philip P. Bliss, "Wonderful Words of Life," *Ibid.*, p. 77.
12. Myron S. Augsburger, *Mastering the New Testament, Matthew*, Dallas, TX: Word, Inc., 1982, p. 322.
13. *Ibid.*, pp. 321-323.
14. William Barclay, *The Gospel of Matthew*, Vol. 2, Philadelphia, Pa: The Westminster Press, 1982, p. 415.

[15] *Ibid.*

[16] Lloyd John Ogilvie, *Silent Strength for My Life*, Eugene, Ore.: Harvest House Publishers, 1990, p. 259.

[17] *Ibid.*

[18] Robert F. Biehler and Jack Snowman, *Psychology Applied to Teaching*, 7th ed., Boston: Houghton Mifflin Co., 1993, pp. 428-430.

[19] *Ibid.*, p. 29.

[20] *Ibid.*, pp. 76-85.

[21] Kenneth N. Taylor, *Words of Wisdom*, Minneapolis: World Wide Publications, 1967, pp. 78-79.

[22] Frank Charles Thompson, ed., *The New Chain-Reference Bible*, Third Improved Ed., Condensed Cyclopedia, Indianapolis: B. B. Kirkbride Bible Co., 1934, p. 48.

Printed in the United States
149506LV00002B/5/P